Cornish Railways

Stop
Start of N.S.T.
section

Previous page: With the insignia on the cab end reflecting the title of this book, No 37207 *William Cookworthy* eases under the narrow road overbridge at the delightful backwater of Coombe Junction while making its way to Moorswater clay dries to collect a loaded china clay train in June 1986. This traffic ceased in 1996 but following a period of closure the line again saw use during 1999 to a cement distribution depot, where infrequent trains continue to call. The second bridge 'aperture' to the left of the locomotive once spanned the abandoned Liskeard & Looe Union Canal. The notice between the arches signifies the start of a 'No Signalling Token' section.

Left: In celebration of the 150th anniversary of the Great Western Railway in 1985 a small number of locomotives were repainted in lined green livery and one of them, Class 50 No 50007 *Hercules*, was also renamed *Sir Edward Elgar*. In April 1986 the pristine locomotive is seen on the main line crossing the imposing Moorswater Viaduct that spans the East Looe River Valley, with an up train. The line in the foreground now terminates at Moorswater but prior to 1901, when a connection was made between Coombe Junction and Liskeard, it was part of the original Looe branch line.

Right: The main railway gateway to Cornwall since 1859 has been across the famous Royal Albert Bridge, which celebrated its 150th anniversary in 2009. The single track structure spans the mighty River Tamar, which it crosses some 100ft above the high water line, a requirement imposed by the Admiralty in Victorian times. The two primary spans are 455ft long, the total length is 2,200ft with ten tall masonry piers on the Cornish side and seven on the Devon side. In April 1987 large logo liveried Class 47 No 47660 enters Cornwall with the then daily Liverpool to Penzance express. In 2011/12 the entire structure was being refurbished.

Cornish Railways

John Vaughan

All photographs taken by the author

Ian Allan
PUBLISHING

Right: The majority of photographs (but thankfully not all) taken by the author in Cornwall during the past 43 years were in monochrome, a situation that continued until the end of the 20th century. Consequently Classes 22, 42 and 43 do not appear in colour within these pages. Hopefully the appearance of a single sepia image as a reminder of the past will not compromise the otherwise all-colour production! On 20 June 1970, when Newquay still boasted its original granite station, multiple platforms and semaphore signalling, Class 42 'Warship' No 831 *Monarch* will shortly be departing for London Paddington (despite displaying an inaccurate headcode), while the local DMU has just arrived at platform 1. The locomotive was withdrawn in October 1971 and the class became extinct on British Railways (BR) the following year.

First published 2012

ISBN 978 0 7110 3467 9

© Ian Allan Publishing Ltd 2012

Published by Ian Allan Publishing

an imprint of Ian Allan Publishing Ltd, Hersham, Surrey KT12 4RG.
Printed in England by Ian Allan Printing Ltd, Hersham, Surrey KT12 4RG.

Visit the Ian Allan Publishing website at www.ianallanpublishing.com

Distributed in the United States of America and Canada by BookMaster Distribution Services

MIX
Paper from
responsible sources
FSC® C014615

Below: In addition to the usual types of standard diesel motive power employed on service trains in the Royal Duchy since 1958, the scene has been enhanced by regular visits of unusual classes of locomotive at the head of railway enthusiast specials and other 'Chartex' traffic. On 22 March 1992 a pair of Southern Region (SR) Class 33 'Cromptons' arrived in Cornwall with the 'Cornish Construction Crompton' special. Nos 33050 *Isle of Grain* and 33063 in new Railfreight triple grey livery are seen here at the unlikely location of Falmouth Docks. The train went on to visit Newquay. Past visitors have been wide ranging, from Class 20s and 40s to Class 55 'Deltics' and 56s.

INTRODUCTION

Based on a synopsis prepared by the author 30 years ago Ian Allan Publishing agreed in 1982 to the proposal to produce a monochrome pictorial railway book featuring what was then contemporary diesel traction on the railway lines of Cornwall, and in 1983 *Diesels in the Duchy* (ISBN 0 7110 1326 8) was duly published. Now it is the publishers who have approached a much older and perhaps wiser author to prepare a similar, primarily pictorial, book but this time in colour and in landscape format. Although a veteran of over 45 books (10 of them featuring Cornwall) prepared over 45 years, this is the author's first British all-colour production, featuring a pictorial potpourri of scenes on *Cornish Railways* over the past four decades.

This volume is not about every yard of Cornish main line and branch line, nor is it a study of every class of diesel locomotive and unit that has ever crossed the River Tamar into Cornwall. *Cornish Railways* is a very personal and selective photographic appreciation of the railways of Cornwall between 1969 and 2012, prepared by an individual who has always had a passion for the county and who has studied the subject in some depth. The only major problem encountered has been deciding which images to exclude! With the exception of a few favourites, the overwhelming majority of photographs either have never been published before or were published only as tiny images. A handful have appeared elsewhere in monochrome, but as an entity the collection is unique.

For those interested in photography, the author's preferred medium for several decades was monochrome film, with colour being very much an occasional afterthought. Gradually more colour film was used and by the end of the 20th century the era of monochrome had ended. Except for the years 1977 to 1983 when two large format Pentax 6 × 7 cameras were used, the photographs appearing within these pages were taken on 35mm Nikon single-lens reflex film cameras, including Nikkormat Ftn, FG20, FE2, FM2 and F301. A range of fixed-focal-length Nikkor lenses have been utilised ranging from 35mm to 300mm, with perhaps 85mm being the norm. Although images were home-processed until the end of the 1970s, later it was specialist processors and more recently photographic laboratories that have handled processing, particularly VPS Imaging of Goring-by-Sea and DNA Photo Imaging of Worthing. The images in this book originate from both Kodak and Fuji colour slide and print film, with film speeds ranging from 64asa to 200asa. None of the photographic images within these pages have been modified by software programmes – apparently a common activity in this digital age, normally to cure fundamental deficiencies.

In an attempt to satisfy most tastes, the final selection of photographs has been something of a balancing act not only between subject, date and location but also between traditional 'three-quarter' views and something a little more progressive, without indulging in unduly contrived compositions. Half of the photographs herein date from the 1969 to 1989 period and the other half from 1989 to 2012. The author has never been 'put off' by the weather and, whether the day brings brilliant sunshine or torrential rain, the camera is never put away during railway photographic safaris. There is no doubt that we all feel better when the sun shines – indeed, nearly two-thirds of the photographs contained herein were taken in sunny conditions – but in Cornwall the weather is very changeable and if a 'fair weather only' approach is adopted, a railway photographer would fail to show the many moods of nature and would produce an unrealistic portfolio, as well as be out of action for much of the time!

This InterCity 125 unit is seen passing from Cornwall into Devon across Brunel's last masterpiece, the iconic Royal Albert Bridge. The photograph shows the juxtaposition of the River Tamar, the town of Saltash in the background and in the distance Coombe-by-Saltash Viaduct. The introduction of High Speed Train units revolutionised services between London and Penzance as journey times tumbled below the five hour mark, although the speed restriction across the bridge is a modest 15mph. It is hard to believe that these reliable streamliners have now been working in Cornwall for over 30 years.

One of the joys of railway photography in Cornwall is the delightful scenery. Until the comparatively recent abandonment of time-honoured standards of lineside maintenance, which has allowed vegetation of all descriptions to totally eliminate what were once excellent photographic vantage points, there had been scores of wonderful vistas to savour across the delightful Cornish countryside. The dramatic contrast in the Cornish scenery is quite a challenge. In eastern Cornwall there are attractive rolling hills, substantial tidal inlets and remarkable valleys, many of them crossed by the railway on impressive viaducts. There are distant views of Kit Hill, Bodmin Moor and Caradon Hill, all interspersed with fields given over to cattle and agriculture as the market town of Liskeard is reached, where passengers change for trains to Looe. The ride down the Glynn Valley to Bodmin Parkway is spectacular, featuring several imposing viaducts. At Bodmin Parkway the preserved line to Bodmin General and

For the vigilant observer there are still plenty of surviving reminders of Cornwall's rich railway history. Artefacts come in all shapes and sizes and illustrated here is a small Great Western Railway (GWR) cast metal cover to a water stop-cock on the down platform at Liskeard station. Many other relics can be found, particularly trespass warning signs, metal castings on overbridges and various items of infrastructure, including station buildings, signalboxes and goods sheds.

Boscarne Junction connects cross-platform with the main line. The River Fowey tumbles along its picturesque path past Restormel down to the wonderful old town of Lostwithiel. Just beyond the station is the Fowey branch, now freight-only down to Carne Point. Once into central Cornwall the evidence of the china clay industry is everywhere to be seen, although the white clay-covered houses and rivers are now a thing of the past and the industry is in decline. The junction station of Par is interesting as passengers change for the Newquay branch line and china clay trains rumble through from time to time. The port of Par can be seen from the train and the depot at St Blazey can be glimpsed, with a short branch line connecting the two.

The major town of St Austell still boasts its GWR overbridge and there is a bus station interchange adjacent to the station. Burngullow is a significant point on the line in that not only is it the junction for the Drinnick Mill freight-only branch line to Parkandillack but it is the limit for china clay train operations on the main line. West of this location the undulating countryside is attractive and agricultural, culminating in arrival at Truro across two major viaducts, with the impressive cathedral as a backdrop. The city of Truro is the capital of Cornwall and it boasts a wonderful old station, the busiest in Cornwall, with deep awnings and semaphore signals. Passengers change here for Falmouth. Contrasting with the china clay country of mid Cornwall are the industrial surroundings between Chacewater and Camborne. This was the primary mining area in the 19th century and many old abandoned engine houses can still be seen. The countryside is rugged, a point emphasised by the almost treeless hills of Carn Brea and the imposing Lord de Dunstanville monument. Redruth retains fine station buildings and awnings, although semaphore signals have been swept away. Camborne station is less attractive but again this centre of the former mining industry has a fascinating history. West of Camborne, rolling hills and farmland dominate the scene as the main line descends past the remains of Gwinear Road station (once the junction for Helston) and past the charming village of Angarrack to Hayle, which was once the home of the remarkable Harvey's Foundry. The old commercial port is now rather dilapidated but the passing scenery is of interest. The views across the Saltings find the north Cornish coast, and the St Ives branch is clearly visible before the junction station of St Erth is reached. There is then a short gallop from the north to the south coast as Marazion is passed, with glimpses of St Michael's Mount. The line follows the coastline to Penzance, which now has the only all-over-station roof in Cornwall. The 75 miles from Saltash to Penzance is a sheer delight with infinite railway photographic opportunities.

One of the immense joys of Cornish railways is the surviving infrastructure. There are 40 railway viaducts of note in Cornwall and these tremendous, largely Victorian, edifices are imposing, often dwarfing the trains that run across them. At many locations it is not just the viaducts that fascinate but the remains of the adjacent piers left in situ following the demolition and replacement of the original Brunel/Brereton examples. Some of the tidal inlets and deep valleys crossed by these viaducts are also spectacular as light, weather and tides conspire to 'make or break' a photograph. Other edifices that appear in Cornwall include engine houses, especially near Scorrier, castles such as Trematon, Restormel and Carn Brea, and a number of tunnels on both the main and the branch lines. Rivers and estuaries can be found in several good railway photographic locations, as illustrated within the pages of this book. The many Cornish branch lines, with their twisting alignment and single track, have a certain charm that can produce fine photographs. All of the Cornish branches are scenic and are well worth exploring with a camera or simply 'riding the train'. Overall, the topography is spectacular and a joy to discover, although it takes many years to cover all of the ground.

Another wonderful survivor in Cornwall is the presence of lower quadrant semaphore signalling, which survives at seven locations. Although the actual number of signals has been rationalised over the years, these wonderful products of yesteryear make superb photographic props and never fail to enhance a photograph. They are also useful in showing that a train is in section and that the camera will shortly need to be raised for action. With the signals come the signalboxes and these can be very photogenic, even those not operating traditional signalling. Most Cornish stations have been modernised, but there are still some original structures, period overbridges, or at least some aesthetic appeal at St Germans, Liskeard, Bodmin Parkway, Lostwithiel, Par, St Austell, Truro, Redruth, St Erth and Penzance. Most other stations on both the main line and branches have been heavily rationalised.

One major problem that present-day railway photographers encounter is a lack of interesting or locomotive-hauled trains. Even in comparatively recent times Cornwall had been noted for a wide variety of such trains, but once IC125 units and, later, Voyagers began to replace locomotives on main line long-distance services, except for the overnight sleepers and the occasional special, their days were numbered. Local services on the main line and branch lines are now entirely in the hands of diesel units with limited variety, although over a period of nearly 50 years the variety of types appearing has been considerable. In times past various van and postal trains, mixed freights and special loads were all locomotive-hauled but most have disappeared, leaving little more than infrequent china clay trains and the occasional scrap-metal, cement or sand train for the diesel engine fan to savour. From dozens of china clay trains per day, nowadays in Cornwall a single locomotive working a rake of CDA wagons on a fixed and infrequent 'circuit' and occasional long-distance freights are likely to be the only locomotive movements, inevitably powered by a Class 66 variant. The classes of diesel locomotive motive power have also dwindled. From the halcyon days of even the 1970s and 1980s, when Classes 22, 25, 37, 42, 43, 45, 46, 47, 50 and 52 could all turn up, the current scene is likely to produce only Classes 57 and 66, with very occasional Class 47 or 67 appearances. From time to time vintage interlopers on enthusiasts' specials liven up the scene. In the future the main interest, in terms of motive power, is going to be largely limited to ever-changing corporate Train Operating Company liveries. If one wants to photograph trains in Cornwall it will also have to be accepted that diesel units are simply part of the everyday scene.

In addition to working railways there are the remains of scores of lines from times past throughout the county, both of standard and narrow gauge, some of which have been closed for decades but are still traceable. The discovery of some railway artefact or even a short section of abandoned rail as a result of some 'bramble bashing' can be fascinating. One must, however, always be aware of the boundaries of private land and seek permission before trespassing. In certain public areas, notably in the Luxulyan Valley and up around the Cheesewring, the remains of granite 'setts' (primitive sleepers) and short sections of track are clear to see and encourage further research regarding where the lines ran to and from, the date they opened and closed, the commodities carried and the type of motive power used.

It is unfortunate that in recent years a number of developments have worked against the railway photographer, even in the depths of Cornwall. The rapid growth of lineside foliage has already been mentioned, but arguably the most negative development has been the growth of a 'health, safety and litigation' culture. Even 30 years ago there were many signalmen who were prepared to have a chat, and on occasions one might be invited into the signalbox without touting for a visit. Sometimes even a cup of tea would be offered! Many of the drivers were enthusiast-friendly and on a number of occasions, while standing around with a camera, I have been asked whether I would like a cab ride. One could ask whether it was in order to wander into a yard or perhaps take a photograph from a siding well away from the main line and the response would almost always be positive with a 'Mind your step' warning. In the days before the internet and mobile phones, the supervisors at St Blazey were usually co-operative in providing information and the allocation of specific motive power to a train was often 'flexible'. Provided one adopted common courtesies, station staff were generally helpful. An unforgettable experience was a ride in the brake van from Bodmin Road to Wenford Bridge, an event enjoyed on at least three occasions before the line closed. Although rarely used, for some of these years I had an official lineside photographic pass, which was easily obtainable from the Western Region, but such

facilities have long since been withdrawn. In any event, over the years the best photographs have been taken from public places, without the need to be on railway property.

There has been a change in attitude towards enthusiasts and non-railway personnel in recent years and for many reasons this has been understandable with an increase in vandalism, the emergence of terrorists within the population and, as mentioned above, the arrival from the good old USA of litigation mania, whereby somebody who trips over a rail sues the railway company for millions. Against this background it is hardly surprising that the railway companies have become less enthusiast-friendly. Another change for the worse has been the demolition of buildings and other infrastructure items and their replacement by aesthetically offensive structures, ranging from buildings resembling concrete boxes or greenhouses to coloured-light signal posts and the visually displeasing palisade fencing. Lineside clutter has also increased along with graffiti, although that, thankfully, is a rarity in Cornwall.

In selecting photographic vantage points in Cornwall there needs to be a trade-off between locations, scenery and the trains that operate. For example, in east Cornwall all main line passenger trains can be observed but there is minimal china clay traffic, with perhaps a single freight train in each direction during daylight hours, a massive reduction compared with times past.

Another surviving railway relic in Cornwall is located at Par Bridge crossing, between St Blazey and Par Docks. Seen in 2009, these manually operated crossing gates are believed to be the last in Cornwall and are used at least twice per week when a china clay train works to the docks area for loading. The restoration of the former crossing-keeper's cottage on the right was featured in a BBC television programme. In the background is the friendly Par Inn, an ancient St Austell Brewery tied public house.

One of the joys and fascinations of exploring and photographing all aspects of Cornish railways and in creating images of current operations, preserved lines or the remains from the past is the dramatic contrast between old horse-worked tramways, such as the remains of the Treffry Tramway, and the newest developments of the 21st century. Space prevents a comprehensive look at railway remains but in this idyllic scene between Wheelpit and the Treffry Viaduct at the upper end of the Luxulyan valley a short section of rail survives, some 80 years after the last horse-drawn wagon rumbled through the woods.

Between Lostwithiel and Par is probably the busiest stretch of line and where the maximum freight traffic, such as it is, can be observed. The line beyond Par to Burngullow can be reasonably productive but the photographer will not see the clay traffic to the large Rocks works at Goonbarrow Junction on the Newquay branch. West of Burngullow, daytime locomotive-hauled trains are so sparse that the weekly fuel-tank train to Long Rock, just east of Penzance, is the only example. On an out-and-back basis that's two photographs per week! This is a remarkable contrast compared with only 30 years ago when there were mixed freights to Truro and Ponsandane, cement to Chacewater, milk from St Erth and numerous postal and van trains from Penzance. On the branch lines it is necessary to differentiate between passenger and freight-only lines, the former enjoying timetabled services but the latter being very 'hit and miss' in terms of traffic. The branch trains are geographically self-contained, requiring a dedicated visit.

The railways of Cornwall are remarkable in their variety and diversity, both past and present. The first tramways, plateways and minor narrow gauge lines to appear in Cornwall were in the mines and pits that were liberally distributed throughout the length and breadth of the county. Most of these lines employed humans, horsepower or ropes and cables to move wagons, but in 1809 the first long-distance tramway was constructed from the man-made harbour at Portreath to the mining district around St Day and Scorrier, over five miles distant. This line was followed by other narrow-gauge horse-operated industrial lines in the 1820s, before the standard gauge Bodmin & Wadebridge line opened in 1834. This was to be the first passenger-carrying railway in Cornwall and the first to employ steam locomotives. The first attempt at building and opening what would later become part of the Cornish main line was by the Hayle Railway in 1836, with passengers being carried between Hayle and Redruth from May 1843. The standard gauge West Cornwall Railway eventually took over and, using part of the Hayle Railway alignment, they were conveying passengers between Penzance and Truro by August 1852. The broad gauge Cornwall Railway main line from Plymouth (and by implication the rest of the UK rail network then prevailing) to Truro opened in May 1859 and, with a change of train at Truro, passengers could travel by rail from London to Penzance. However, it would be 1867 before passengers could travel the length of Cornwall in the same railway carriage. The line from Truro to Falmouth was to be part of the CR main line but almost from the opening in 1863 it became secondary to the Truro to Penzance route. The entire Cornish main line was eventually taken over by the Great Western

Railway and in 1892 they converted the whole of it and all broad gauge branch lines to standard gauge, abolishing the broad gauge forever.

Between 1836 and 1920 a large number of branch lines were built throughout Cornwall. These were built to both standard and broad gauge. Some of these lines carried passengers, mostly but not entirely from the main line to important towns and villages, while others were constructed purely to serve various industrial sites and areas mainly for the conveyance of minerals. One of the earlier lines which finally opened throughout in 1846 was from Caradon and the Cheesewring down to Moorswater, near Liskeard, where the head of a canal that ran down to Looe was located. One of the more impressive networks was that of the Cornwall Minerals Railway that took over the old Treffry Tramway lines built between 1841 and 1857. The CMR finally connected the north coast at Newquay with Par and Fowey on the south coast. There were several associated CMR branches and sidings. The CMR opened in 1874 and was wholly taken over by the GWR in 1896. GWR branch lines in Cornwall that were over a mile in length served Launceston, Looe, Bodmin, Wadebridge, Fowey, Newquay, Carbis Wharf, Carbean, Lansalson, Drinnick Mill, Meledor Mill, Falmouth, Newquay (from Chacewater), Treamble, Newham (Truro), Portreath, Tresavean, Helston, Hayle Wharves and St Ives, plus many other minor lines and long sidings.

In addition to this remarkable GWR network the former London & South Western Railway/Southern Railway lines in Cornwall must not be forgotten. In addition to the old Bodmin & Wadebridge Railway route to Bodmin North, Ruthern Bridge and Wenford Bridge, southern lines included Padstow, the entire North Cornwall line, Bude and Callington branches, the last three mentioned being partly in Devon. These southern lines in Cornwall have now all closed with the exception of the stub from Calstock to Gunnislake, which remains open for passengers.

While the Cornish main line remains intact, albeit rationalised in places, the same cannot be said for the branches and minor lines. Some of the tramways closed during the mining depression during the mid 1860s while others, such as the Treamble to Gravel Hill line, succumbed to later recessions in the 1880s. Other lines closed by the end of World War 1 included the Redruth & Chasewater Railway, the Pentewan Railway and the Looe & Caradon Railway. Although between the two World Wars there were closures, such as passenger services between St Blazey and Fowey, the main period for closures occurred in the so-called Beeching era of the 1960s when dozens of passenger and freight-only lines, sidings and stations closed. Some primary examples of

Penryn station on the mainly single line Truro to Falmouth branch once boasted a passing loop but that was abolished in the 1970s, leaving just a single platform and waiting shelter (see page 136). However in 2009/10 there were exciting developments when a passing system was introduced using just a single extended platform. On the right unit No 153372 has just arrived from Falmouth Docks in April 2010 and will shortly head for Truro, while on the left No 153368 enters the station with a down train. This new arrangement makes it possible to provide a half hourly service, the best since the line opened 149 years ago, as a result passenger journeys on the branch have almost doubled.

withdrawn passenger services on former GWR lines include Bodmin General, Fowey (from Lostwithiel), Newquay (from Chacewater) and Helston. Not only did the branch lines suffer but former GWR main line stations at Doublebois, Grampound Road, Chacewater, Scorrier, Carn Brea, Gwinear Road and Marazion also closed. Following the 1960s 'Reshaping Plan' the closure process, particularly for freight-only lines, continued. For example, Wadebridge in the 1970s, Carbis Wharf, Ponts Mill, Wenford Bridge, Roskear, Hayle Wharves and the Retew branch in the 1980s, Trelavour, Nanpean and Drinnick Mill lower in the 1990s and Crugwallins in the 21st century. Add all of these closures together and there are an awful lot of Cornish railway remains to be discovered.

Another category of railways in Cornwall are the preserved lines, which operate both steam and diesel trains on both standard and narrow gauge lines for the pleasure of the public, especially in the peak tourist season. Top of the list must be the Bodmin & Wenford Railway which operates trains between Bodmin General and both Bodmin Parkway and Boscarne Junction. They have a wonderful fleet of steam and diesel locomotives. Other popular lines include the Launceston Steam Railway, which operates narrow gauge trains over a short section of old branch line at

This interesting study shows the modern scene at Liskeard on 5 April 2009. First Great Western IC125, with power car No 43026 trailing, is forming the 09.50 Penzance to Paddington while a Cross Country liveried unit, with power car No 43285 leading, runs past with an empty stock working. However, it is almost amusing to see this modern hardware beneath manual lower quadrant semaphore signalling of a bygone age, one of the surviving delights in parts of the Royal Duchy.

gauge trains from Benny Mill to the East Wheal Rose (mining) area, where there are other miniature railways (the route includes a short section of the old Chacewater to Newquay branch); and the Helston Railway Preservation Society, which has been formed to run trains over a short section of the old Helston branch line from their base at Trevarno. There are many miniature lines at centres of public entertainment, such as Newquay Zoo. All of these lines present photographic opportunities, although sadly, with a single exception, there has not been space to include them within these pages.

For readers wanting more information, may I mention these other books I have written:

An Illustrated History of the Cornish Main Line (ISBN 978 0 86093 625 1), Ian Allan/OPC 2009, for a detailed pictorial history of the Cornish main line.

Branches & Byways: Cornwall (ISBN 0 86093 566 3), Ian Allan/OPC 2002, for a detailed history of Cornish branch lines.

Diesel Days Devon & Cornwall (ISBN 0 7110 3040 5), Ian Allan 2005, for a survey of the various classes of diesel that have worked west.

An Illustrated History of West Country China Clay Trains (second edition) (ISBN 0 86093 543 0), Ian Allan/OPC 1999 (first edition 1987), which deals comprehensively with the subject of china clay trains.

Rails to Newquay (ISBN 0 8536 1677 1), Oakwood Press 2008, or *The Newquay Branch and its Branches* (ISBN 0 86093 470 5), Haynes Publishing/OPC 1991, for a detailed history of the Newquay branch and associated lines.

Transport and Industrial Heritage: Cornwall (ISBN 978 0 7110 3372 6), Ian Allan 2009, for a broad appreciation of the industrial and transport history of Cornwall.

Diesels in the Duchy (ISBN 0 7110 1326 8), Ian Allan 1983, for a pictorial survey of the Cornish railway scene in the British Railways 'blue' era.

Tramway to Newquay (ISBN 978 0 9522190 1 9), Photrack 2011, for a pictorial history of the old Newquay Tramway.

I have many happy memories of the past 43 years of railway photography in Cornwall. I have been blessed to have had the company of several loyal and long-term friends. I have met some really great railwaymen and many friendly 'locals' over the decades but sadly many of those have now 'gone on'. I have seen the most wonderful natural sights in all types of weather and spent hours waiting for non-existent freight trains! I have sought interesting locations and taken thousands of photographs, immersed myself in libraries and centres of learning and worked my way through the most wonderful collections of books and pictures. I have even downed a few pints of Cornish bitter beer at some fairly quaint establishments. This land of legend with its remarkable history and magnificent scenery was shared by my ancestors and I consider it to be a very special place. With due modesty I am delighted to say that my 43 years of photography, authorship and study have been recognised by the Cornwall County Council's 'Cornish Studies Library' in Alma Place at Redruth and they have agreed to house my monochrome collection of Cornish railway photographs for posterity. It is known as 'Cornwall Centre – John Vaughan Collection', and it is now available to the general public for viewing and research. With the publication of *Cornish Railways* in my 70th year I have decided to retire from railway publishing and, as a result, this will be my 48th and last book. This is an extremely gratifying end to a very special episode in my life. I hope you enjoy *Cornish Railways* – a colourful photographic railtour of the Royal Duchy of Cornwall.

John Vaughan

Goring-by-Sea, Sussex
May 2012

The first station in Cornwall, working down the main line from east to west, is Saltash. Since the mid 1980s there have been 'Welcome to Cornwall' signs on the platform and in the current examples First Great Western and Cornwall County Council have collaborated to ensure the signs are bilingual, although how many passengers will understand the expression 'Kernow a'gas dynnergh' from the ancient Cornish language is unknown. Passing the disused but extant upside buildings is a sleek Virgin Voyager with an up inter-regional train in October 2006.

Although minds naturally focus on the Royal Albert Bridge as the only rail route into Cornwall, in years past there were 'border' crossings on the Bude and Launceston (GW) branches, in addition to the North Cornwall line from Halwill Junction to Wadebridge, but most of these lines closed in the 1960s. The only other railway crossing from Devon to Cornwall to survive spans the River Tamar at Calstock and is part of the Gunnislake branch. Crossing the magnificent 870ft long, 120ft high and 1907-built Calstock Viaduct with a Gunnislake to Plymouth working is a Regional Railways Class 150 diesel unit in April 1995. An inflatable craft, a jetty, a swan and some ducks complete the charming scene.

In addition to GWR lines in Cornwall there was also a significant London & South Western/SR presence, especially in the north of the county. The branch line from Bere Alston to Callington was a latecomer, not opening throughout until 2 March 1908. The line opened under the auspices of the Plymouth Devonport & South Western Junction Railway using part of the alignment of the narrow gauge East Cornwall Minerals Railway. From 6 November 1966, in the post-Beeching era and by then under the control of the WR, the Callington to Gunnislake section of the branch line was closed, leaving the latter station as the terminus. With the green and white SR sign prominent the crew of the branch DMU have a chat in front of the Col Stephens style of corrugated tin station building before returning to Plymouth in March 1969, the author's first ever railway photograph in Cornwall.

The remainder of the Gunnislake branch line was again under threat of closure but the difficult terrain between Devon and Cornwall at this location and the problems encountered in travelling by road to Plymouth saved the line. However, the branch was further rationalised in the early 1990s when the terminus was moved several chains nearer Plymouth to enable a low railway bridge over the A390 road to be removed. This view shows the sad remains of what had once been the island platform at Gunnislake in April 1995 and should be compared to the photograph opposite.

Following the closure of the Wadebridge and Wenford Bridge freight lines in 1978 and 1983, the short section of track from Calstock to Gunnislake became the very last railway line in Cornwall with SR origins. The remainder of today's branch line from Calstock to Plymouth via Bere Alston is of course in the county of Devon. The branch line survives and is now marketed as 'The Tamar Valley Line' by the operators First Great Western. There are nine round-trip workings per day with one fewer on Saturdays. There is a Sunday service in the peak summer months, with a single journey time of 45 minutes. Posing at the new functional Gunnislake terminus on 6 April 2009 is Class 153 single car unit No 153370.

The first of over 30 viaducts of substance on the Cornish railways is Coombe-by-Saltash, which is 86ft high and comprises seven arches, each with a span of 70ft. The original curved viaduct was replaced in 1894 and the track here was doubled in 1906. Sporting yellow snowploughs, Class 50 No 50037 *Illustrious* looks really impressive as it heads the 13.40 from Paddington to Penzance across the structure on 31 March 1986. In the background is the old Saltash goods yard and shed, last used in 1963.

The number of freight trains running on Cornish metals during the past decade has significantly decreased. In times past there could be up to half a dozen non-passenger workings into and out of Cornwall per day, but now this can be as meagre as a single daylight train. Many freights have paths but rarely run, such as Freightliner Heavy Haul 6Z66 FO-Q Burngullow to Angerstein Wharf sand train (the material being a by-product of the china clay industry). Fortunately on 5 October 2007 this erratic working was caught on camera leaving Coombe-by-Saltash Viaduct hauled by No 66622. Some of these trains travel to Bow in East London and much of the material conveyed was used in the construction of buildings for the 2012 Olympics.

One of the many delightful tidal creeks in East Cornwall is at Forder where a substantial viaduct crosses the valley. While waiting to photograph a train, with the tide coming in, it is possible to experience a strange phenomenon where the ground appears to be sinking into the water!

Above the remains of the ancient Anthony Passage tide mill, a two-car Class 150 in Wessex Trains maroon 'pictogram' livery scuttles by with a Penzance to Plymouth stopping service in September 2008. Just visible top left is the local landmark of Trematon Castle.

One of three viaducts built on a new 1908 main line alignment from Wearde Quay to St Germans is Forder Viaduct, which is 699ft long and 69ft above the high water mark. Crossing the masonry and brick structure across Forder Creek on 12 August 1987, with a 'flash' of sunshine brightening an otherwise cloudy scene, is No 50038 *Formidable* with a Paddington to Penzance train comprised of InterCity liveried stock. The 16-cylinder English Electric Class 50s were operational in Cornwall for nearly two decades.

The viaduct across the River Tiddy at St Germans is spectacular, especially when seen from ground level at the attractive quay on the west side of the inlet or from this location on the A374 Torpoint road, just over half a mile to the south. Although taken from one of the best photographic vantage points, the help of a medium telephoto lens is required to fill the frame.

Photographed on 11 September 2007, just before Virgin Trains lost their Cross Country franchise to the Arriva Company, now owned by Deutsche Bahn, one of their aesthetically attractive Voyagers is seen crossing the magnificent 1908 structure with the 09.30 Penzance to Glasgow working.

The combination of prevailing southwest winds and the associated weather fronts that drive the warm Gulf Stream across the Atlantic Ocean have a significant impact on the Cornish climate. The weather is wetter, sunnier and warmer than in many parts of the UK. There is more than 1mm of rainfall on 155 days of the year (50% more than London) totalling over 1,042mm or 41in per annum. There are only 14 days of frost, half as many as London, and over 1,703 hours of sunshine per annum (16% more than London). In photographically recording Cornish railways and the surrounding scenery, one encounters ever-changing climatic conditions that produce dramatic contrasts in lighting, atmosphere and moods. With rain in the air and with damp, bleak stone walls in the foreground, these ancient buildings look gloomy, if not sinister, as the down 'Cornish Riviera', the 10.06 ex-Paddington FGW IC125, crosses St Germans Viaduct on its way to Penzance on 17 May 2008.

Another 1908 build on a new main line alignment is the impressive curved eight arch 618ft long Lynher Viaduct (sometimes called Nottar Viaduct, a name carried by the original structure some 900 yards to the south). Powering over the River Lynher at precisely 16.15 on 20 October 1988 is all blue Class 47/4 No 47476 with a Carne Point, Fowey to Tavistock Junction train comprising 19 new CDA wagons. These would be loaded at ECC's Marsh Mills installation. By this date locomotives were being fitted with headlights and all blue Class 47s were becoming less common. The class has been active in Cornwall for well over 35 years.

Other than for local workings in Cornwall, one normally associates 'long distance' services with London, Paddington, the Midlands, the North East of England, and Scotland. However, over the years there have been scheduled services to other areas including the SR, for example from Penzance to Waterloo, Brighton and Portsmouth. Until axed in December 2009, one intriguing service continued, a Sundays only 13.50 through train from Penzance to Waterloo, operated by South West Trains. In its 'alien to Cornwall' livery SWT Class 158 two-car unit No 158865 descends from Trerulefoot to St Germans with the up working on 5 April 2009. The barren hills of Dartmoor can be seen in the far distance.

Colourful Cornwall is a justified expression along many of the railway cuttings in late spring and early summer as the yellow flowers of the gorse bushes contrast with the vibrant colours of the native rhododendrons. Position one of the delightful single 'bubble' car diesel mechanical units between them in glorious sunshine and the result can be quite pleasant. No 55012 is seen just east of Tresulgan Viaduct with an up local from Liskeard to Plymouth in June 1989. Note the roof ventilators and the twin exhaust pipes taking spent gases above the roof line.

It is only in retrospect that one realises what a wonderful era the 1980s were in Cornwall with locomotive-hauled trains comprising mostly Mark 1 rolling stock. In those days everybody could get a seat and have the guarantee of being adjacent to a window, with plenty of luggage space and scope for natural ventilation. It seems beyond belief that, performance aside, modern designers did not have the acumen and ability to provide such basic facilities in the uncomfortable and poorly designed Pendalinos and Voyagers of today's world. The greed of the TOCs in cramming more and more seats into carriages 'airline style' means that one can spend 400 miles stuck behind a pillar facing backwards in an 'airline' seat. With the sound from its 16 cylinders reverberating around the Cornish countryside near Doddycross, No 50004 *St Vincent* looks magnificent as it heads towards Penzance on a fine April day in 1986.

An early start to the day on 5 April 1986 was rewarded by this backlit shot of No 37196 in original Railfreight livery and carrying the totally Cornish name of *Tre Pol and Pen*. The train is heading west at Trerulefoot with a Newton Abbot to Lostwithiel train of clay hood wagons containing ball clay from the Heathfield branch in Devon. Ball clay wagons could be identified by a thin yellow band around the base of the tarpaulins that covered the wagons. From 1974 a raised metal frame was fitted to most wagons so that the covers did not come into contact with the clay, and rain water easily drained away. The resulting shape gave rise to the expression 'clay hood'. The clay in these wagons would end up at Carne Point, Fowey, for shipment.

One of the finest structures in East Cornwall is the 795ft long and 138ft high Coldrennick Viaduct. During an 1897 rebuild there was a terrible disaster here when a working platform collapsed, sending 12 men crashing to their deaths in the valley below, 25 children being orphaned by the incident. Crossing the structure on 13 June 1987 with the 07.00 Milton Keynes to Penzance is original Network SouthEast liveried No 50019 *Ramilles*. Note the brick extensions on the masonry piers, which finally replaced a part timber structure in 1898. Menheniot station is located at the west end of the viaduct, the least used Cornish main line station.

When introduced in 1989 the new traffic flow conveying china clay slurry from Burngullow to Irvine in Scotland was the longest freight haul in the UK and it became known as the 'Silver Bullet', but by June 1997 there was not much silver to be seen on the by-then grubby bogie tankers. Having just crossed the 113ft high Bolitho Viaduct, Transrail No 60062 *Samuel Johnson* heads 'up country' with its liquid load for use in the paper-manufacturing industry. The Class 60s first appeared in Cornwall in 1995, replacing pairs of Class 37s on long-distance freight trains. The locomotives later carried the popular nickname of 'Tugs'.

The Class 60s were the last all British-built main line diesel locomotives ordered by British Rail(ways). A total of 100 locomotives were constructed between 1989 and 1993. Having survived sectorisation the entire fleet was absorbed by English, Welsh & Scottish Railways (EWS), a subsidiary of the American Wisconsin Central Railroad. EWS eventually placed a significant order for 250 General Motors locomotives, putting the Class 60s in a vulnerable position. By the start of 2010 only five were left in service, although the number later increased. Some were repainted in EWS livery, such as No 60048, seen here in truly diabolical 'golf umbrella' conditions near Bethany with the up 'Silver Bullet' train 6B88 09.40 Burngullow to Irvine on 10 June 1998. In 2011 it was announced by EWS successor DB Schenker that up to 20 of the class would be refurbished, extending their life by up to 10 years.

In this fun picture from June 1998 the Looe branch diesel unit is dwarfed by the 150ft high Liskeard Viaduct that carries the main line across the valley to the east of the town. The Regional Railways Class 153 is descending from Liskeard's branch line station (located at right angles to the main line station) down to Coombe Junction, where it will reverse before continuing to Looe. Again note the brick extensions that replaced an upper wooden 'fan' structure in 1894, the Gothic apertures in the brickwork and the tie rods. The steel girders replaced earlier iron examples in 1929.

By April 1990 a number of Class 50 express passenger locomotives had been relegated to civil engineers trains working out of Plymouth Laira. One such machine was No 50019 *Ramilles* that was also repainted locally in all-blue livery. With the town of Liskeard forming the backdrop the English Electric Type 4 heads vacuum braked four wheelers containing old ballast over Bolitho Viaduct on the up road. Liskeard station is visible top left. The locomotive was preserved and in 2012 was active on the Mid Norfolk Railway.

In the author's experience, the sight of double-headed Class 66s is a rarity in Cornwall. However, on a delightful evening in September 2002, the late afternoon air-braked freight from St Blazey produced super power in the shape of No 66237 and what was believed to be No 66115, seen here just east of Bolitho Viaduct. One locomotive could easily have handled the 720-tonne load and the train was on time, so the double heading must have been for operational reasons. The outskirts of Liskeard can be seen in the top right-hand corner of the photograph.

Although by design only a handful of special trains are illustrated within these pages, Class 52 'Western' diesel hydraulic No D1015 *Western Champion* is one of the exceptions. This truly remarkable locomotive, beautifully maintained by the Diesel Traction Group, is one of a class of the best-looking diesels ever produced in the UK. Featuring twin high-speed Maybach engines, together delivering 2,700hp, the machine looks good and sounds great. Properly maintained, it shows what the class could have been capable of, if BR had adopted similar servicing standards as the preservationists. On 5 April 2009 the maroon machine crosses Bolitho Viaduct with a special Chartex returning to London. Earlier in the day it had rescued a failed steam-hauled special – payback time for some Class 52 failures in the early 1960s?

There is nothing more evocative than photographing the last 'daylight' train of the day in conditions such as this and then spending the evening reflecting on the day's activities with a friend over a pint of Cornish real ale. On 12 June 1987, as the sun slowly sinks behind the hills of Bodmin Moor, the 18.35 Penzance to Bristol Temple Meads is seen crossing Bolitho Viaduct a little after 20.00 hours behind large logo No 47481. This precise view has now been obliterated by tree growth owing to a lack of lineside maintenance, but then the locomotive-hauled 'Bristol' no longer runs.

Taking advantage of the initial descent from Liskeard to Moorswater Viaduct before the long climb up to Doublebois, this 2,700hp Class 50 is producing plenty of 'clag' from its four exhaust ports as it heads into the sunset on a July evening in 1986, with the Liverpool Lime Street to Penzance working, comprised mostly of air-conditioned Mk 2d stock. Notice both up and down signals on the same side of the track at this location, a leftover from the days of steam, and note also the scars of the lifted up side sidings on the right, now a car park.

The storm clouds are brewing over Bodmin Moor as train 1A19, the famous 11.00 ex-Penzance 'Cornish Riviera Express', comprising a splendid rake of mostly Mk 2b coaches, departs from Liskeard for Plymouth and Paddington behind No D1016 *Western Gladiator*, in March 1974. An additional five coaches will be added at Plymouth North Road. The class were regular performers in Cornwall for 15 years before the withdrawal of the last of the class of 74 locomotives in February 1977. The dark sky shows off the white electrical conductors located on the incredibly tall telegraph posts, long since removed. The foreground sidings were also removed many years ago but on this day old civil-engineer wagons filled with redundant sleepers were being stored thereon.

Liskeard remains a bastion of semaphore signalling even though the number of 'pegs' has been reduced in recent years. The surviving 1915 signalbox now communicates with Plymouth panel in the up direction and Lostwithiel on the down, but back in March 1974, when this scene was recorded, it was St Germans and Largin respectively. In foul weather train 1A98 (which should perhaps be 1B98 – from London) arrives at the market town behind one of the 2,700hp Class 52 diesel hydraulics. Note the delightful stubby up starting signal in the 'off' position and the connection with the Looe branch beyond.

As a regular visitor to Cornwall one soon learns that the holiday brochures featuring sunny coves and a glowing coastal path are often the work of fiction and that the county is not always conducive to conventional, fair-weather 'sun over the shoulder' railway photography. Keeping the camera working on an appalling day in February 2008, one of the less usual diesel unit variants in Cornwall, Class 150/1 No 150127, forming a down late-afternoon local service arrives at Liskeard in the gloom with only the headlight, reflection and the warm glow from the signalbox windows giving any cheer. This recent transferee to the FGW TOC would soon be repainted.

After the rain comes the low cloud and swirling mist, which on this November day in 1996 completely enveloped the Liskeard area for several hours. Arriving at Liskeard's branch line station, which, as already mentioned, is set at right angles to the main line station, and with its headlight trying to penetrate the fog is single car No 153305 with a service from Looe.

The station was recently renovated and new chocolate-and-cream GWR/BR(W) signs were provided. In the summer the site is heavily used by 'park and ride' travellers who wisely do not attempt to park their cars in the popular but crowded coastal town of Looe but instead ride 'The Looe Valley Line'.

Far left: The beginning and the end of the day can often be the best times for railway photography, especially if sometimes the conventional 'three-quarters front, sun over the shoulder' approach is ignored. In April 1986 the morning stopper from Plymouth to Penzance comprised three air-conditioned coaches and a BG van. In this era local trains were always grossly overpowered with a Type 4 locomotive on the business end. This Class 50 is seen at about 07.50 between the up and down main line semaphores, while crossing Liskeard Viaduct. The line in the foreground is the connection to the Looe branch and the Moorswater freight line: note the 5mph speed limit.

Left: From time to time it is worth photographing passengers (without which there would be no railway) with the actual train being secondary to the composition. In October 2007 a member of the platform staff at Liskeard is engrossed in conversation with one of at least 10 passengers on the down platform. Braking to a standstill is silver Alphaline liveried Class 158 No 158751, forming the 06.58 Bristol Temple Meads to Penzance and offering about 130 seats. Class 158 appearances in the Royal Duchy are now relatively infrequent.

At the very end of the day, after dinner and with the camera back in the bag, it was always a pleasurable experience to retire to the platforms of Liskeard at about 21.00 to simply view either the up 'Travelling Post Office' thundering through the station with a Class 50 in full cry or to wait for the St Blazey to Stoke-on-Trent air-braked freight at about 22.30, which normally produced a pair of Class 37s. Especially on a still night, these trains could be heard miles away. Not wanting to use the flash at night for safety reasons, a 30-second time exposure of the up TPO produced an interesting effect. The headlight matched the alignment of the white platform edging while the 'tracers' left by the headcode panel lights on a Class 50 are clearly visible. The wet platforms add to the atmosphere.

There is no doubt that the majority of railway enthusiasts and photographers prefer locomotives to unit-based trains. However, the reality is that, except for the 'Night Riviera', all main line and all branch line passenger trains in Cornwall are now in the hands of various types of multiple unit, with only the very occasional freight train breaking the mould. However, with clean IC125 units passing lower quadrant semaphore signals, attractive photographs can still be secured. An immaculate FGW unit, with power car No 43196 leading, arrives at Liskeard from Penzance with a Paddington-bound train on 5 April 2009.

In railway photographic circles it never ceases to amaze that new but everyday sights seem, in retrospect, to pass into history at the blink of an eye. This photograph is one of very few taken of a buffer-fitted Virgin liveried HST power car, but only a decade or so ago they were commonplace. A total of eight power cars were modified in this way during 1987/8 for use with

Class 91s on the East Coast main line. An up inter-regional service from Penzance is seen entering Liskeard station in September 1998, headed by power car No 43068. In this early privatisation view the former InterCity stock has yet to receive the attention of the paint shop. Note the old, soon to be replaced, bullhead rail on both up and down main lines.

39

One of the author's earliest colour shots in Cornwall was this view of an all-blue Looe-bound single power car calling at Coombe Junction on 2 March 1969. The old shelter and sign were still in GWR chocolate-and-cream colours. The line on the left is the freight line to Moorswater which once doubled as part of the run round loop. At this time the main line across Moorswater viaduct could clearly be seen. In this post-Beeching branch line era the passing 'Warship' diesel hydraulics were largely ignored! John Blamey's old woollen mill at Lamellion Bridge in the background has, sadly, since been demolished.

This view shows the motive power provided for the Looe branch in the summer of 1974, in the shape of Swindon two-car DMU No P554. The unit is about to change direction for the run down to Looe and the train guard can be seen carrying the oil tail lamp to what will now be the back of the train. The driver is also changing ends but from 1981 when the signalbox was closed and fewer trains called at the diminutive station the driver changed ends by walking through the train.

After the signalbox closed, the freight line on the left was lifted and both passenger and freight trains shared the single track, which was controlled by two ground frames. The train guard or shunter had communication with Liskeard signalbox, the telephones being located in small lineside huts. In this unusual view taken on 22 April 1987 both passenger and freight trains populate Coombe Junction. Four-wheeled Class 142 railcar No 142027 is about to depart for Looe with the 09.08 from Liskeard while No 37175 waits for the road to Liskeard with a train of clay hoods.

This dramatic contrast at Coombe Junction was taken in September 2004, some 35 years later than the view aside, top left. The train is still a single car unit but a more modern Class 153 diesel hydraulic, while the foliage has completely taken over, obscuring the local road bridge and the distant viaduct. The hut has been replaced with another and there is no trace of the lifted freight line alignment. The one salvation is perhaps that the line is still open. To celebrate the 175th anniversary of the GWR a special steam and diesel shuttle operated along the Looe branch in September 2010.

In addition to Looe branch workings, china clay trains shared the section of line from Liskeard to Coombe Junction until 1996, when English China Clay's Moorswater works stopped drying clay. After approximately three years of disuse, cement trains started to use the line, albeit on an erratic basis. In April 1987 large logo No 37175 looked quite splendid as it made its way between leafless trees towards Moorswater with a long rake of empty clay hood wagons. The locomotive had 'self steering' bogies that reputedly reduced flange wear. The old Liskeard and Looe Union Canal alignment can be seen on the left, which substantially pre-dated the railway.

One of the benefits of sectorisation in the mid 1980s was the arrival of new liveries, which made such a refreshing change from years of BR corporate blue. Creeping across the minor road just outside of the ECC Moorswater works at 08.15 on 6 May 1989 is new Railfreight liveried No 37673. The road is without warning lights or barriers and a member of the train crew had the job of looking out for road traffic. The CDA clay wagons would end up at Carne Point, Fowey, the old clay hoods all having been withdrawn the previous year. A couple of hundred yards outside of the works, beneath Moorswater Viaduct, is a run-round loop that now enables incoming cement wagons to be propelled along the single track and into the works after the locomotive has changed ends.

As mentioned on the previous page, after the clay works closed, the line to Moorswater remained disused for a number of years but with the track in situ. Eventually in 1999 some of the buildings were used for the delivery, storage and distribution of Blue Circle cement products, now owned by Lafarge. Initially this was delivered from Earle's sidings in Derbyshire but later trains originated at Westbury before reverting to Earle's again in recent years. In September 2004 old Cornish cottages fill the foreground as Freightliner's 126-tonne 'Heavy Haul' locomotive No 66613 leaves the works with empties, a remarkable sight at this remote Cornish backwater.

One of the more dramatic shots secured on the Looe branch was in March 1974 when a terrible storm was raging over the Liskeard area. However, 'bubble' car No P118 (55018) found only sunshine at Sandplace as it ambled down to Looe. These single car units were active in Cornwall for over 30 years. To compete with the old canal from Moorswater the railway opened here in 1860 for goods and in 1879 for passengers but by then the canal was reported to be silted-up and overgrown. The canal did not finally close until about 1909 and today there are but a few traces of Victorian engineering left as a reminder of those halcyon days.

The Looe branch runs down the valley of the East Looe River, broadly parallel with a minor road and the old abandoned canal. As already mentioned Looe is jammed with traffic in the summer months and the railway operates a 'park and ride' system with motorists being encouraged to park at Liskeard station and take the branch train to the attractive little town. Passengers are rewarded with a picturesque run such as this section of track at Terras Crossing, south of Sandplace. Looe-bound three-car DMU No 117305 is approaching Terras Pill beside the estuary in September 1993. After giving over three decades of service in the county of Cornwall the old diesel mechanicals were at the end of their days by this time. It was therefore quite refreshing to see one of the old girls repainted in GWR chocolate-and-cream livery but with BR 'lion and wheel' transfers still running in the summer of that year.

A further view at Terras Crossing, just a short distance from Looe, shows the tidal nature of the waters at this point. Wading into the river to obtain this shot is a precarious business when a good pair of Wellington boots is as important as film in the camera! In April 1995 a Regional Railways Class 153 unit makes for Liskeard. The Looe branch was fortunate to survive the Beeching purge of the 1960s as it was once scheduled for complete closure but narrow roads and heavy summer loadings resulted in its survival. The Train Operating Company is now FGW.

The time gap between the introduction of sectorisation and the withdrawal of the old vacuum-braked clay hood wagons was approximately two years and so photographs of Class 37s in Railfreight livery hauling the little wooden bodied four-wheelers are less common. Sparkling from a recent repaint on 24 July 1986 is No 37696 seen crossing from the up to the down main line at Liskeard with a load of china clay from Moorswater. A total of 775 of the wooden bodied wagons were built at Swindon between 1954 and 1960, based on an old GWR design, but by this date there were only about 450 remaining in service. Following withdrawal in 1988 most of the clay hoods were scrapped by Coopers Metals at Sharpness Docks.

The 147ft high Moorswater Viaduct was completely rebuilt in 1881. However, what is particularly interesting are the remains of some original piers with their Gothic apertures, on the down, or south, side of the line. Such an example can be seen just left of centre. Crossing the impressive structure during a sunny period in April 1986 is No 50046 *Ajax*, on the point of the 07.30 Penzance to Glasgow. In the valley far below is Moorswater works, where china clay was conveyed by pipeline in slurry form from Parsons Park on Bodmin Moor (some four miles distant) for drying.

On rare occasions freak weather conditions can make or break a photograph; however, the circumstances on this April day in 1987 were particularly unusual. The entire day had been grim with dark clouds and little light. Nevertheless, despite being an erratic runner in terms of precise timings the weekly Dover to Goonbarrow Junction train of empty Polybulk wagons was due.

As the train crossed Moorswater Viaduct a shaft of sun suddenly appeared between two clouds and in a 'flash' of a few seconds illuminated the locomotive, a handful of wagons and part of the viaduct. After a rapid tweak of the aperture ring all-blue No 47343 was photographed heading west with a train that had originated in mainland Europe. The gloom soon returned!

Sited below the mighty St Pinnock Viaduct in the beautiful Glynn Valley of the River Fowey is the Trago Mills retail complex which, although something of a blot on the natural landscape, attracts the crowds and provides valuable local employment. With its buildings dwarfed by the 1859 structure of the Cornish Railway the modern scene is depicted as EWS Class 66 No 66119 glides effortlessly across the structure as it climbs from Bodmin Parkway towards Doublebois with the now discontinued up 'Silver Bullet' china clay slurry train in May 2005.

Left: The climb from Bodmin Road (now Parkway) to Doublebois is spectacular in terms of gradient, scenery and the succession of viaducts. St Pinnock Viaduct, seen here, is the tallest in Cornwall at 151ft. As will be apparent from the granite extensions to the masonry piers, the viaduct was rebuilt in 1882 and in 1964 the track across it was singled to save expensive girder renewal work. Using its available 4,500hp, a London-bound IC125 in original blue and yellow livery rides high on 17 April 1985. Until recent times the plantations of conifers had obliterated most of the railway photographic vantage points in this area.

Below: The recent felling of trees in the Glynn Valley has opened up some new vistas for railway photography. On a bleak 25 June 2011 Direct Rail Services Class 20s Nos 20308 and 20309 pass the up 'Cornish Riviera' just west of Largin Viaduct as they head train 1Z37, a Spitfire Tours Mazey Day chartex from Gloucester to Penzance.

Above: The Bodmin & Wenford Railway operates trains between Bodmin General and Bodmin Parkway, and Boscarne Junction. The lines had closed to passengers in 1967 and to freight in 1983 but after the formation of a preservation society in 1984 passenger services recommenced in 1986. In addition to a splendid GWR/LSWR collection of steam locomotives the B&WR also has a fine collection of diesels. Making a guest appearance at a 1991 diesel gala was Class 35 'Hymek' diesel hydraulic No D7017, a type that appeared in Cornwall in limited numbers in 1964/5 but which otherwise was rarely seen in the county. The class of 101 locomotives became extinct on BR metals in 1975. The Type 3 is about to leave Bodmin Parkway, with its 1,700hp 16-cylinder Maybach engine smoking well.

Right: In June 2011 the Bodmin & Wenford Railway celebrated the 25th anniversary of its first public service train. On 25 June 2011 16-cylinder English Electric Class 50 No 50042 *Triumph* in BR blue livery starts its climb away from Bodmin Parkway over speed-restricted track and heads for Bodmin General. Until 1990 the locomotive was a regular performer on the nearby Cornish main line.

Of all the classes of motive power that have appeared in Cornwall and the West Country since dieselisation the Class 52 'Westerns' undoubtedly had the largest fan base. By the time of their final demise their followers developed almost cult status as special after special was organised to satisfy an insatiable thirst. In this unusual and rarely recorded view, captured just before dawn at about 05.00, when most railfans would still be in the horizontal, one of the 'Whizzos' has just arrived at Bodmin Road with the down 22.25 postal train from Paddington. In the up platform is the daily goods for Wadebridge headed by Class 25 No 25223 that had just arrived from St Blazey. The illuminated cab and overbridge enhance the scene, captured on 9 May 1975.

Another 'blast from the past' is this typical impression of train steam heating, which did not completely disappear from our railways until the mid 1980s. The Class 52 diesel hydraulics were fitted with steam-generating boilers but often there were leaks from the steam pipes between and beneath the ageing Mark 1 coaches, typified by this study at Bodmin Road. Also on 9 May 1975,

No D1071 *Western Renown* is heading the down 23.45 overnight train from Paddington to Penzance in the early morning gloom. The locomotive was one of the few fitted with an additional cab ventilator: notice the small square aperture just below the windscreen.

The Wenford Bridge goods ran daily Monday to Friday but during the 1970s it often ran thrice weekly, and prior to closure of the line in September 1983 services were 'as and when required'. As I had formally arranged with BR to travel on the train and been supplied with a permit, the train crew could not have been more cooperative regarding photography, including a slow speed run past! In those relaxed days travel was permitted on the footplate and in the brake van. In this scene No 08377 approaches Helland with a box van, three china clay wagons and the mandatory brake van. Note the 'Southern Railway' warning sign.

The working of the Wenford goods was a leisurely affair with a booked departure time from Bodmin Road of 09.00 and a return at 14.00. Including the journey to and from their St Blazey base, the total round trip exactly equalled a single shift for the driver, second man and guard/shunter. On occasions, owing to the many reversals, the crew would not always place the brake van at the back of the train, which made sense between Bodmin General and Road because it avoided a complex shunt. Having stopped short of the station on a downhill section of track and having detached the locomotive, the 'train', comprising a single wagon and a brake van, was left to run down to Bodmin Road by gravity using the manual brake in the brake van to control the movement! The view dates back to March 1974.

In the 1970s the Wadebridge goods was rarely photographed because it ran in total darkness for much of the year. It left Bodmin Road early morning at 05.25, returning at 07.15, thereby leaving the line free for the following Wenford Bridge freight. The brake van and goods wagons were normally propelled from Bodmin Road to Bodmin General to avoid run round before working 'locomotive first' to Wadebridge. At about 06.15 on a dull morning and with the shunter in attendance No 25223 reverses up to the stop blocks at Wadebridge with two wagons. After attaching the brake van the train will shortly depart from the old SR site. Note the disused crossing gates in the background across the old closed and lifted line to Padstow. This area is now covered in tramac.

The Class 25 diesel electrics arrived in Cornwall to replace the unsuccessful North British built 1,000/1,100hp Class 22 diesel hydraulics in about 1970. Although delivering only 1,250hp the BR/Sulzer Type 2s were more powerful and more reliable than the D63xx locomotives and they were perfectly adequate for lighter freight trains on the minor branch lines. Here No 25223 is seen at the splendidly named Grogley Halt, which had closed to passengers eight years earlier, with a Wadebridge to Bodmin Road freight on 9 May 1975. The payload included slate dust from Delabole, which was transferred to road haulage when the line finally closed in 1978 and taken out of use in January 1979, the trackbed becoming the 'Camel Trail' leisure facility. The blue discs refer to a small group of enthusiasts from Sussex who were travelling in the brake van.

There was no greater joy in Cornwall than to arrange or cadge a ride on the Bodmin Road to Wenford Bridge goods. Part of the route dated back to 1834, which was the first standard gauge railway line in the county! The full round trip from St Blazey Yard included nine reversals; twice at St Blazey, Bodmin Road, Bodmin General, and Boscarne Junction respectively and once at Wenford plus a splendid ride through the woods bordering the River Camel. The motive power during the last 20 years of the ancient line's life was invariably a 350hp Class 08 shunter. In this March 1974 shot a tired-looking No 08839 is framed by the overbridge at Bodmin General while taking a lunchtime breather. The Boscarne (and formerly Padstow) line is in the foreground.

This scene depicts the very rare sight of a snowfall in Cornwall. Although more common on the higher moorland, snowfalls sufficient to cover the track are unusual on the main line. In this seasonal Christmas card view, taken on 19 January 1985, the 07.50 Bristol Temple Meads to Penzance, running 50 minutes late owing to the adverse weather, leaves a wintry Bodmin Road behind a grubby No 50018 *Resolution*. On this occasion the passengers will no doubt be grateful that these Mark 1 coaches are electrically heated! A broadly equivalent train still runs as a two-car DMU!

The 'Maybach organs' will be shouting as this venerable Class 52 diesel hydraulic emerges from the 'clag' on the climb up to Bodmin Road in March 1974 while powering 4M05, a heavy perishables and parcels train from Penzance to Crewe. The withdrawal of such trains was a major loss for railway enthusiasts and for the coffers of Cornish railways. The train is passing between old-fashioned speed-restriction signs, indicating limits of 65mph on the down line and 50mph on the up road. The down signal appears to be neither 'on' nor 'off'. Note the sidings in the up yard on the right now the location of a B&WR carriage shed, while the old abandoned down yard on the left is now a car park.

Over the years chartex special trains have brought a bewildering array of diesel locomotive classes to Cornwall but Class 31s have always been one of the less usual locomotive types to traverse Cornish metals. This pair of 50 year old locomotives were not showing their age on 25 June 2011 as Nos 31601 and 31190 rushed non-stop through Bodmin Parkway with special train 1Z20 from Tame Parkway to Penzance, organised by Pathfinder Tours. The leading locomotive is in the appropriate 'Devon & Cornwall Railways' livery. It would appear that a visit from the weedkiller is long overdue.

Before the foliage took over, the road bridge just south of the ancient Respryn Bridge over the River Fowey, to the west of Bodmin Parkway (Road), was a good, if traditional, location to photograph up morning or down evening trains. By 1988 the vacuum-braked clay hood wagons had disappeared from the Cornish railway scene and these 50-tonne (gross) air-braked CDA wagons had replaced them. Initially 124 such wagons were delivered, which were broadly based on 'merry-go-round' HAA coal wagons but with a special lining and covers. With 20 wagons in tow No 37674 is about to start its long climb towards Liskeard on its way to Moorswater during the summer of 1989.

With the reduction in china clay production in Cornwall any additional freight activity is welcome. An erratic but sometimes weekly freight flow, contracted to Freightliner, is sand traffic from Burngullow. The material is a bi-product of the china clay industry. The loaded train is so heavy that it is split into two parts, which depart from Burngullow at 11.00 as 6C59 and 17.45 as

6A59 behind a 'Heavy Haul' Class 66/6. The trains run initially to Hackney Yard at Newton Abbot and then the combined train makes for Reading and various terminals in the home counties (see page 15). On a delightful April evening in 2010 No 66624 threads the valley of the River Fowey below Restormel with loaded bogie hoppers.

In glorious countryside near Respryn Bridge the annual weedkilling train is seen spraying the up track in the spring of 1994. Based at Horsham in West Sussex, the Chipman's company train was well travelled in the south and west of England, powered by a pair of Hunslet-Barclay 1,000hp Class 20s in the Class 20/9 sub-class, in this case Nos 20901 *Nancy* and 20904 *Janis*, nominally allocated to Kilmarnock. By topping and tailing the train, run rounds were avoided, a great bonus on single track branch lines. Note the old-fashioned headcode discs. The use of Class 20s for this purpose ended in 1998 and the locomotives were sold to DRS early in 1999. Just out of sight to the left of the photograph is the short Brownqueen Tunnel.

Rapidly approaching Lostwithiel in October 1987 and finding a sunny period despite the stormy skies is the 09.30 Paddington to Penzance. Lostwithiel's outer home-signal is 'off' and indicates that the train has a clear road on the down main line, while the smaller semaphore signal is protecting the down goods loop. This was the era when liveries were ever changing, the Class 43 power car having received new InterCity branding while the coaches remain in BR grey and blue with white InterCity transfers. Above the signal gantry are the remains of the ancient Restormel Castle, a local historic landmark that is well worth visiting.

Truly a diesel in the landscape, before the foreground and distant fields were converted into Lostwithiel golf course, all-blue No 47066 heads the morning 09.35 St Blazey to Severn Tunnel Junction 'Speedlink' service on 4 April 1986. The train is heading towards Restormel, with the town of Lostwithiel in the left background. A Danzas wagon and two VTG Ferrywagons head the formation and they will end up in mainland Europe. All wagons in the consist will contain various products of the Cornish china clay industry. Through the leafless trees on the right the River Fowey can just be glimpsed, just a couple of miles from the point where it meets the sea.

Back in the 1980s it was a pleasure to simply sit on a hillside above what was to become Lostwithiel golf course and watch and photograph passing trains. There was an excellent view in both directions but following commercial development and a remarkable growth in vegetation it is now impossible to even see the railway line. Under a typical Cornish sky on a glorious day in

June 1986 No 37207 *William Cookworthy* (the discoverer of china clay in the West Country) drops down the Fowey Valley towards Lostwithiel with a long rake of clay hood wagons from Moorswater. In addition to the already mentioned ruin of Restormel Castle, top left, the large white building on the right is Restormel Manor.

The Class 37s were active in Cornwall for over 20 years, from 1978 when they started to replace the 1,250hp Class 25s, until 2000 when Class 37 replacement by GM Class 66s commenced in earnest. One of the less common Class 37 liveries in Cornwall was 'Mainline', a mid-blue sometimes referred to as 'Aircraft blue'. In this June 1998 photograph Nos 37055 *RAIL* and 37274 power away from Lostwithiel with just three 80-tonne Polybulk wagons in tow, forming a late afternoon St Blazey to Exeter Riverside freight. The line on the right is the up goods loop while on the extreme right is the siding for the old dairy where thousands of gallons of milk and dairy produce were once loaded for conveyance by rail.

Ancient and modern subjects over a century apart are depicted at Lostwithiel in September 2008, with both remaining as part of the current railway scene. Providing a dramatic contrast are the 1893-built Victorian signalbox, which still manually controls rail movements in the area, and a high-tech North American-built General Motors (GM) Class 66 diesel locomotive.

Another contrast is provided by the signalman who is handing over not only the time-honoured single-line token for use on the single track branch line to Carne Point, Fowey, but also a newfangled mobile communications device. No 66004 heads a rake of loaded CDA wagons away from the up goods loop, an event that has now been reduced to one or two workings per day.

The Class 37s or 'Siphons' were a great favourite of railway enthusiasts west of the River Tamar between 1978 and 2000. They were ideally suited to the china clay scene with a useful power band, a reasonable route availability and reliability figures to be admired. The St Blazey train crews knew what the power handle was for and sound recordists knew that a Class 37 getting under way with a heavy clay train or climbing one of the many gradients on Cornish railways was a very special sound. In appalling conditions in June 1998 a commendably clean No 37673 in Transrail livery has the brakes applied as it arrives at Lostwithiel, having won the battle of the climb up to Treverrin tunnel with 1,000 tonnes behind her. As a matter of interest Class 66s can take 1,900 tons in their stride on the Cornish clay 'circuit'.

No 37675 *William Cookworthy* (a name formerly carried by No 37207) looks stunning in the afternoon sunshine as it rounds the curve at Lostwithiel station with a down air-braked freight bound for St Blazey in August 1987. The locomotive is in original Railfreight livery and included in the load are brand new CDA clay wagons that would soon replace the ageing vacuum-braked wooden bodied clay hoods. Note the semaphore signals and the clay covered sidings; in recent years the latter have, sadly, become disused because block load trains from fewer installations do not need to be shunted or marshalled.

The old 1859 Cornwall Railway works at Lostwithiel had been partly derelict for many decades when photographed in June 1996. Indeed part of the building complex had been gutted by fire. With the old glassless rusting metal window frames emphasising the dereliction, Transrail liveried No 37674 *Saint Blaise Church 1445-1995* passes on the down main line with the inevitable china clay empties. The buildings were later incorporated in a new development of apartments and town houses, Transrail was absorbed by EWS and the Class 37s were mostly pensioned off: such is progress!

One of the new liveries that emerged from the sectorisation of BR was the so-called 'Dutch' livery, which was applied to Civil Engineers Departmental locomotives. Seen here berthed in the up freight loop at Lostwithiel on 8 October 1993 is No 37207 of the DCWA (Departmental Western) Pool with half of the Dover to Goonbarrow Junction train, comprising 11 empty Polybulk wagons.

Running between clay hoods and the down side signal gantry on the left and a banner repeating signal on the right, with a Penzance to Bristol train on 19 August 1985, is No 45135 *3rd Carabinier*, one of the long extinct (on BR) 2,500hp 'Peak' Class 45/1s fitted with electrical train heating. When introduced in May 1961 the locomotive was numbered No D99. Within just eight weeks of this picture being taken 'Peaks' were banned west of Bristol, bringing to an end sightings of the class in Cornwall. This locomotive was one of only eight Class 45/1s to be preserved, presently on the East Lancashire Railway, although as many as 16 'Peaks' across the Class 44 to 46 range have survived the cutter's torch.

Late afternoon lighting highlights passenger and freight workings at the down end of Lostwithiel station in September 2004. The 13.35 Paddington to Penzance, here headed by power car No 43036, had the distinction of being the only down London train of the day to stop at Lostwithiel, while in the background No 66115 waits for the ground disc signal to be pulled off before leaving the now abandoned sidings and continuing its journey down the branch line to Carne Point with china clay for the docks. Both liveries are already redundant, with First Great Western having come up with a less imaginative and certainly less attractive colour scheme and EWS now having been taken over by the Deutsche Bahn subsidiary DB Schenker who also have their own house colours.

The standard motive power for current Cornish main line stopping train services is one of the ubiquitous two-car Class 150 DMUs. There is a limited ability to strengthen these trains owing to the non-availability of spare stock and during peak periods the units are frequently run with standing room only. FGW have refurbished most of its fleet and the majority are now in the company's new colours. These colours contrast with the gardening efforts of Network Rail staff as No 150246 departs from Lostwithiel with the 09.34 Exeter St Davids to Penzance on 5 June 2009.

One of the most charming and tranquil locations for observing trains in the whole of Cornwall, albeit at a distance, is the hamlet of St Winnow on the banks of the River Fowey, a couple of miles south of Lostwithiel. Especially on a sunny morning and when the tide is high, the view across the estuary is superb. When no trains are running it is a place for quiet contemplation.

In this view on 22 August 1985 double-headed Class 37s in the shape of No 37207 *William Cookworthy* and 37181 make for Carne Point with clay hoods. A problem now arising is the paucity of traffic, with sometimes only a single train passing in the daylight hours before noon.

As is the case with most of the photographs contained within these pages, they cannot be repeated, and in this instance it is not just that the Class 37 and the wagons that have been reduced to molten metal and matchwood but that this area is now covered by deep undergrowth and quite mature trees. Making a glorious sight beside the River Fowey in the autumn of 1985 is No 37181, seen approaching Lostwithiel Park along the single track branch line with up clay empties. Note the Cornish Railways insignia on the bodyside comprising a BR arrow and Cornish lizard.

Transrail No 37673 passes the ancient Fishermans Arms at Golant in June 1997 with a rake of CDA wagons bound initially for Lostwithiel. The sign on the telegraph pole warns the public that the road is liable to be flooded at high tide!

The lovely old fishing village of Golant on the banks of the River Fowey is understandably over-photographed but it is a scenic location that is hard to resist. When the tide turns, the small harbour slowly fills with water which can produce reflections of any infrequent freight train that happens to pass by. The local public house, the Fisherman's Arms, is a convenient waiting room for the railway photographer hoping to see such a train! No 66019 travels along the causeway between the River Fowey and the village with a massive load of china clay bound for Carne Point, the only train to pass the spot on this October afternoon in 2007. The road by the harbour is liable to flood during spring tides.

The 'dead end' of Carne Point is seen here in July 1986 with redundant Class 10s rotting in the open and being attacked by salt-ridden air. However, there was light at the end of the tunnel in this case as Blackstone-engined No D3452 was preserved on the Bodmin & Wenford Railway at Bodmin General and after much restoration work returned to traffic. Note that the shunter is standing on an ancient wagon turntable. Class 08 shunters replaced the Class 10s and they now conduct shunting movements on the waterfront. EWS have conducted experiments using remote control equipment but to date drivers have not been dispensed with!

It would be inappropriate not to include at least one elevated photograph of Golant and its tiny harbour on the banks of the River Fowey in a book on the railways of Cornwall. A high level view appeared over a quarter of a century ago in *Diesels in the Duchy* and since then the location has become one of the best known in the county. This delightful late afternoon scene dates back to 3 October 1985 and shows driver Don Tregaskes in action with Nos 37222 in blue and 37196 *Tre Pol and Pen* in original Railfreight livery hauling northbound clay empties along the freight only line. There was a tiny halt at this location until passenger services were withdrawn in 1965.

Although passenger services on the Lostwithiel to Fowey line ceased back in 1965 the enterprising Lostwithiel Chamber of Commerce hired a special train to enable members of the public to traverse the scenic freight only line on a few summer Sundays in 1994 and 1995. On 24 September 1995 No 150239 is beautifully reflected in the River Fowey at Golant as it returns to Lostwithiel, watched by an elderly boat owner. Increasing costs prevented a repeat performance in later years.

This photograph of a Penzance to Paddington express descending into Lostwithiel from Treverrin Tunnel during May 1986 was included in *Cornish Railways* because it was headed by grey-roofed large logo-Class 50 No 50042 *Triumph*. After withdrawal this locomotive entered the world of preservation and is now a resident of Cornwall at the Bodmin & Wenford Railway (see page 53). The locomotive was rededicated at Bodmin during 2009 and is a regular performer at diesel galas. In the foreground is the Fowey branch line.

This action profile gives a really good impression of the difference in levels of the main line and the Fowey branch just to the southwest of Lostwithiel. Climbing hard up the 1 in 57/72 gradient during April 1985 is No 37207 *William Cookworthy* as it slowly makes its way up to Treverrin Tunnel on its way to Par. The shunter is riding in the rear cab while keeping an eye on the trailing clay hoods. Again the Cornish lizard is visible around the BR logo. A total of 45 Class 37s have so far been preserved, No 37207 being amongst them and which is located at the relatively nearby Plym Valley Railway.

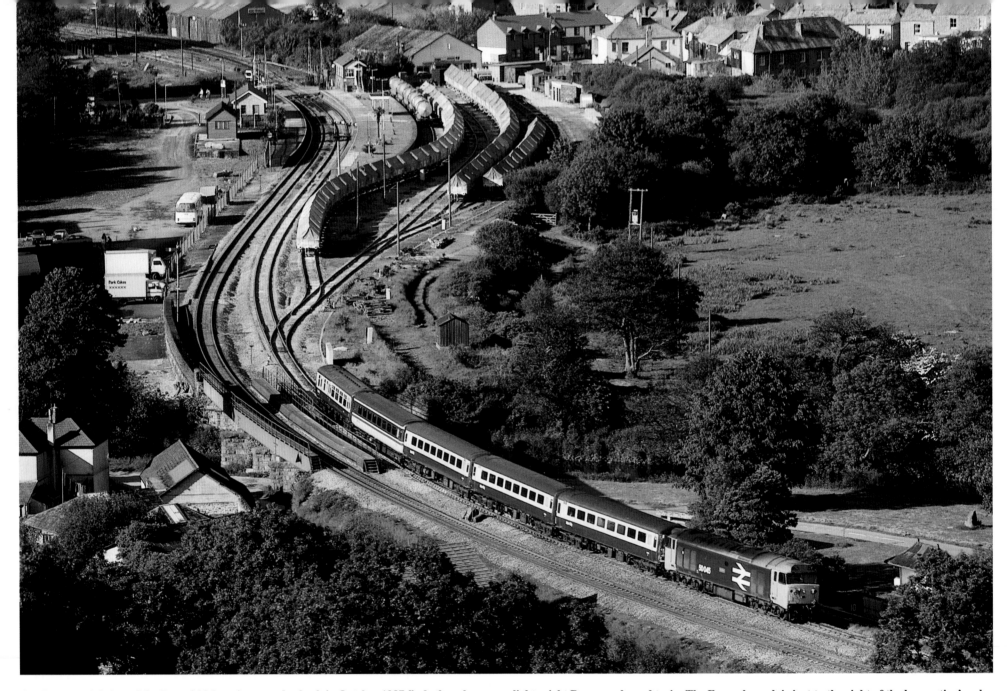

An almost aerial view of the Lostwithiel station complex back in October 1987 finds three long rakes of the soon-to-be-replaced clay hood wagons and a handful of six-wheeled milk tankers located in the down sidings. The up side sidings, the old broad gauge goods shed and the original station buildings have all been swept away. Passing aloofly by is No 50045 *Achilles* with a lightweight Penzance-bound train. The Fowey branch is just to the right of the locomotive's cab but until 1972 the branch had its own dedicated track across the River Fowey, evidence being visible above the InterCity-liveried coach.

With the town of Lostwithiel forming a magnificent backdrop, large logo No 37175 gets to grips with a long haul of empty clay hoods as it slogs up the climb to the summit at Treverrin on its way to St Blazey and Goonbarrow Junction in April 1987. Originating at Carne Point, Fowey, the train will have reversed in one of the goods loops at Lostwithiel with the locomotive running round its train, causing the signalman to lower his barriers three times; inbound, run round and outbound. On the extreme right is the unsightly and short-lived modern dairy building that aesthetically blighted the valley but which was eventually demolished. Happily this locomotive has been preserved at the far-off Bo'ness & Kinneil Railway.

In late afternoon light this long rake of empty four-wheeled clay hoods has a certain symmetry as it descends past Treesmill towards Par behind large logo No 50043 *Eagle* in May 1986. The Class 50s were dual braked and working these wooden bodied vacuum braked wagons presented no problems. The 'Hoovers', as they were nicknamed, were essentially express passenger locomotives with a 100mph capability but on these occasions 40mph would be the norm. Occasionally, especially after works or depot attention, they could be found heading china clay traffic in the Duchy of Cornwall to demonstrate that fault rectification had been successful. From the photographers perspective such appearances were always something to get excited about and looking back over 26 years it is easy to see why.

Heavily backlit by the late afternoon sun and with the brakes applied this all-blue 2,580hp Class 47 No 47240, heading another lengthy rake of clay hood wagons, has just passed Treesmill and is seen below the village of Tywardwreath as it descends into Par. The focal length of the camera lens has captured the entire train in the frame, more by luck than judgement! Note the time-honoured practice of mounting the oil tail-lamp on the last wagon. In years gone by, before the fitting of continuous brakes, such trains had to be stopped at the summit of steep declines for the brakes to be 'pinned down' to prevent runaways, the reverse procedure of 'picking-up' the brakes taking place once the track levelled-out.

One of the most unusual trains on the Cornish main line was the heavily speed-restricted Class 08 working from St Blazey to Bodmin Road and Wenford Bridge and return. The shunter normally left its loads either at Boscarne Junction or Bodmin Road to be 'tripped' by a much larger locomotive, the Class 08 running light with a brake van in tow along the main line section. With its coupling rods flailing at its maximum 15mph, a path has been found for the 'famous' No 08113 and its brake van as they descend past Treesmill on their way to Par and St Blazey in June 1982. The 'fame' was attributable to the Graham Farish company, who marketed an 'N' gauge model of this precise locomotive.

While slumbering on a hillside high above Treverrin Tunnel in April 1986, courtesy of a local farmer, the camera was ready for a down train. However, it was an unscheduled rumble in the tunnel that was heard, which heralded an up train. Within a split second it was realised that the Royal Train was on the move and so a 'grab' shot was attempted. Fortunately a standard lens was fitted to the camera and a brief sunny period flashed across the landscape injecting colour into the green GWR150 liveried Class 47 locomotive (believed to be No 47500 *Great Western*) and the immaculate maroon 'Royal' stock, normally stabled at Wolverton.

This colourful double header is not quite what it seems as NSE liveried Class 50 No 50001 *Dreadnought* is hauling No 37674 'dead in train', which is the 15.01 St Blazey to Gloucester of 3 February 1988. The Class 37 was probably en route to Laira for repair. The train is leaving Par and will be climbing all the way up to Treverrin Tunnel. Over the years up air-braked freights from St Blazey have variously worked to Severn Tunnel Junction, East Usk, Cliffe Vale, Warrington, Sittingbourne, Alexander Dock Junction, Irvine, Mossend, Tavistock Junction, Hackney Yard, Gloucester, Exeter Riverside and Dover, for destinations in Italy and Switzerland. Notice the distant clay tips on Hensbarrow Downs at the very top of the photograph.

The Class 50s were constructed by the English Electric Company at their Vulcan Foundry works at Newton-le-Willows in Lancashire during 1967/68. The locomotives were initially leased to BR and they primarily worked on the West Coast main line north of Crewe. However, as electrification of that line progressed the fleet were gradually transferred to the WR where they worked for nearly 20 years. The fleet of 50 locomotives played an important part in replacing the Class 52 diesel hydraulics, which could not operate in service with electrically heated air-conditioned stock. Such stock is seen here sweeping into Par headed by No 50019 *Ramilles* with the Penzance portion of a train from Paddington in May 1986.

Heavy snowfalls in Cornwall are quite rare but in accordance with the overnight weather forecast this was the winter wonderland that greeted travellers at Par station at dawn on 19 January 1985. With the snow covering the sleepers the 07.30 Penzance to far-off Aberdeen has just come to a standstill. In the background at the outer face of the up island platform is the Newquay branch DMU, which will shortly depart for the 'Surf Capital of England'. Road traffic was paralysed until later in the day but the trains kept running, if a little late. In this unrepeatable image the driver is leaning out of the cab of No 50015 *Valiant* awaiting the 'right away'.

Here we see an exemplary example of precise time keeping at Par on 31 January 2012. The time is 14.45.15 and the Rocks to Carne Point clay train hauled by No 66127, visible in the distance, was due to pass at 14.45.00 while the 13.53 Plymouth to Penzance local on the right comprising No 150126 was scheduled to depart at 14.46.00. The lady in the foreground later said she was 'leaving Cornwall for the last time', hence the large amount of luggage, which certainly enhanced the composition!

Above: There is plenty of information in this view of Par with a mileage post, speed restriction sign, HST carriage stop signs, ground disc signals, lower quadrant signals and a signal number identifying sign all visible. Sweeping across from the down main line to the up main and about to run through the island loop on the left is No 66171 with Carne Point to Goonbarrow Junction CDA empties on a dull day during 2010. The haulage capability of these 126 tonne 3,300hp locomotives has produced trains weighing twice as much as yesteryear working the local china clay 'circuit', resulting in far fewer trains. The Class 66s have a useful 1,440 gallon fuel tank and a quick engine oil change will result in a bill for 202 gallons! On the right is Par goods loop.

Right: On rare occasions the railway photographer is the beneficiary of good fortune. In October 2007 Colas Rail were the proud owners of their first two refurbished Class 47/7s, which were hastily despatched from Eastleigh works to Par to haul the seasonal Railhead Treatment Trains. The author was, by chance, on hand at Par to witness their arrival in Cornwall for the very first time. Looking absolutely stunning in orange, yellow and black livery is No 47749 *Demelza*, which after the removal of the 'Stop' sign will back onto its wagons. Again semaphore signals contribute to the composition. Fittingly this locomotive was formerly No D1660, 47076 and 47625 *City of Truro*, a case of welcome back to Cornwall!

Even though this semaphore signal gantry at Par has been spoilt by a new 'Health and Safety' cage there is still plenty of aesthetic appeal in this 2012 shot. With the signalbox on the left and manual 'pegs' all around London Midland City liveried No 153333 arrives with the 13.03 from Newquay on 31 January. The main lines are to the left of the signalbox.

Even in the best regulated of circles accidents happen from time to time but only on rare occasions would an incident close a complete branch line for two days. Early on 9 June 2010 train 6C99, the 21.47 Newport to St Blazey, was being propelled back into BZ Yard when the rear bogie of a JIA wagon decided to travel back to Par, demolishing two signals in the process. A breakdown crane was summoned from Bescot and the Newquay line reopened on 11 June. St Blazey signalbox is in the right background.

Twisting curves, check rails and a 5mph speed limit make an interesting picture between Middleway Crossing and St Blazey yard. In September 2003 Spanish-built by Alstom but GM-based EWS Class 67 No 67024 has just pulled forward to the closed St Blazey station lower quadrant starting signal with a Rail Express Systems (RES) postal train, which it will now reverse into the yard for servicing. The girder bridge across the River Par dates back to 1874 and the Cornwall Minerals Railway.

As the Class 60s celebrated their 20th birthday during 2009 their popularity was at an all-time high, partly owing to their dwindling numbers. Initially troublesome, with BR taking over a year to formally accept early examples into the fleet following fault rectification, they settled down in revenue-earning service. The class have appeared in many colours but in September 1998 it was a great surprise to find one of only two British Steel Corporation liveried Class 60s at St Blazey in deepest Cornwall. No 60006 *Scunthorpe Ironmaster* is seen shunting a dead No 37521 *English China Clays*, while the local 'Gronk' No 08953 looks on and the BZ shunter hangs on! The livery was short-lived with Corus taking over BSC, resulting in another locomotive repaint.

St Blazey depot dates back to 1874 and the Cornwall Minerals Railway. The brick structure was built with nine distinct bays, each of which was designed to house two tank locomotives coupled 'back to back'. Access to the bays was via a turntable on classic roundhouse principles. In the days of steam the depot had the allocation code of '83E' and in the later diesel era its code was 'BZ'. In this remarkable if not unique view from June 1986 the three primary classes of main line motive power in Cornwall happened to be on display with Classes 47, 50 and 37 in three adjoining 'stables'. The locomotives are Nos 47214, 50043 *Eagle* and 37104.

After 113 years of operation the depot buildings at St Blazey were feeling their age and parts of the structure became unsafe. On 22 April 1987, just two days before operations ceased, No 37196 *Tre Pol and Pen* is 'put to bed' at the end of the working day. The bays were later repaired and converted into small individual industrial units thus ensuring the survival of the Grade 2 listed buildings, designed and built by Sir Moreton Peto. By 2007 the site was barely used by EWS who had transferred most of their operations to Carne Point, Fowey.

Although the old St Blazey roundhouse closed in 1987 the actual depot continued to be an important location for a further 20 years. Locomotives were stabled and refuelled at BZ but not formally allocated thereto. The turntable remained in service for turning locomotives or stock, a facility often used when steam-hauled special trains are visiting the Royal Duchy. Although the site now sees little use compared with times past, there is still a modicum of wagon marshalling and a holding area for trains scheduled to run later in the day. In this June 2009 image No 66115 waits behind the turntable for its path to Stoke-on-Trent. Train 6B99 the St Blazey to Alexandra Dock Junction will reverse out of the yard before pulling forward to join the main line at Par.

As a result of privatisation of our railways and the bidding process for various franchises the American Wisconsin Central Railroad was successful in acquiring a major chunk of British Railfreight operations. Formed in 1996, the company adopted the name of English, Welsh & Scottish Railways, known simply as 'EWS'. Their chosen livery was red and gold, although with all yellow cab ends the colour scheme looked more like red and yellow. Early repaints included an ampersand ('&') within the company abbreviation, as seen here. No 37668 is seen at Middleway on the Newquay branch with a load of CDA wagons from the Rocks works at Goonbarrow Junction in June 1997.

A remarkable survivor in Cornwall is the freight only line from St Blazey to Par Harbour. Traffic is erratic and now comprises only the occasional, normally weekly, train of china clay. The weed-covered single line passes under the Cornish main line, visible in the background. Passing the vibrant yellow flowers of the gorse bushes on the approach to Par Bridge crossing on 8 April 2009 is heavily backlit 126-tonne GM 'Shed' No 66172 with a rake of 80-tonne bogie wagons. For several decades the standard motive power for this working was a humble Class 08 diesel shunter. Note the crowded cab and grass covered sleepers. In 2012 the train normally operated as a Thursdays only working.

Since 1979 the Newquay branch has been the only Cornish branch line to receive long-distance through trains from distant locations during the summer months. Until October 1987 such trains were locomotive-hauled and a typical example is seen here. On 12 June 1987 No 50036 *Victorious* is seen passing the very basic Luxulyan station with the 09.25 from Newquay taking holidaymakers back to Newcastle upon Tyne and many points in between. This is another view now obliterated by tree growth, preventing the casual observer from seeing the trains, the old cottages, the washing line or the runner bean poles!

These facing photographs show Newquay summer holiday trains spanning a period of 35 years! During an all-line railrover in June 1974 the front seat was 'bagged' in the Par to Newquay DMU. These units were very popular with the public compared with the old compartment coaches used on local services in the steam era. A good view of the line ahead could always be had, unless a spoilsport driver lowered the blind! This train was stopped at the outpost of Goonbarrow Junction waiting for an up train to pass via the loop on the right. Gradually train 1M95, the 08.45 SO Newquay to Manchester service, came into view headed by one of the Class 52 'Westerns' but the number was unfortunately not recorded. Adjacent to the site is Rocks works, then owned by English China Clay and now owned and operated by Imerys. Most of the sidings here were (and still are) covered by a thin layer of china clay.

Hundreds of hours have been spent tracking down the peak period holiday trains on the Newquay branch during the past 40 years. The destinations and the motive power have changed significantly over the decades. Once locomotive workings stopped at the end of the 1987 season, IC125 units took over. Nevertheless, the sight of 125mph machines crossing ungated crossings at 5 or 10mph and averaging less than 25mph for the 20¾ mile journey is fascinating. Changes in TOCs and liveries have been the focus of attention in recent years and an innovation in 2009 was the appearance of National Express trains (successors to GNER), which were being hired by Arriva Cross Country. The former company later ran into franchise difficulties. No 43295 was a long way from the East Coast main line as it passed the lightly used station of Roche on 30 May 2009, with the 15.20 Newquay to Newcastle upon Tyne. Fewer than four passengers per day use Roche station.

Above: The wooden-bodied clay hood wagon in the sidings on the left had just a few days of service left when photographed on 5 February 1988. The tarpaulins stretched over the hood frame were attached to the wagons by expandable rubber cleats that were hooked to the wagon sides. Leaving Goonbarrow Junction with an air-braked freight, with three Tullis Russell wagons to the fore, is No 37674 in original Railfreight livery. The wagons had been loaded at the adjacent ECC Rocks works. Although now superfluous commentary, in the 1980s the distinction between vacuum- and air-braked trains and the braking capabilities of the locomotives that hauled them was very relevant. To left of the signalbox is the stack of the closed Wheal Henry china clay kiln.

Right: One of the most fascinating branch lines in the whole of Cornwall was the one-mile-long Carbis Wharf branch, which latterly served only the Goonvean Company's Great Wheal Prosper clay kiln. Opened by the Cornwall Minerals Railway in 1874 the line survived until August 1989. By that time workings were approximately monthly and securing a picture of a train was something of a challenge. Furthermore the condition of the track was giving cause for concern. Early on a September morning in 1988 No 37674 has run along the weed-covered track to deposit a 32-tonne PGA wagon at the little works, the last coal-fired clay-drying installation in Cornwall — witness the stockpile of coal on the left. The chimneys on the right belong to the closed Carbis Brickworks.

Left: This photograph illustrates one of the reasons for slow average speeds on the Newquay line; the many ungated minor road crossings such as that at Quintrell Downs, seen here. A Cross Country voyager unit emerges from a tunnel of trees with a Sunday Plymouth to Newquay service on 7 September 2008. The unit would return as the 11.34 Newquay to Manchester Piccadilly. A year earlier similar units traversed 'The Atlantic Coast Line' but in the livery of Virgin Trains, which was then the TOC.

Right: This shot shows the modern scene at the 136-year-old St Columb Road station, which until 1878 was called Halloon. The alloy and glass 'bus shelter' is a recent addition, having replaced old brick-and-wood buildings that were demolished many years before. Some 40 years earlier there had been a passing loop, signalbox and goods yard at this location but now only a single line and platform grace the site. On a very bleak summer Saturday in 2008 an 'XC' Arriva company Voyager unit is seen passing with the 15.22 Newquay to Manchester. There is no local service on the branch on summer Saturdays.

The Class 46 'Peaks' were real workhorses in Cornwall, performing genuine mixed-traffic duties and working Class 1 express trains one day and Class 7 freights the next. Eventually Plymouth Laira had an allocation of the locomotives. The class had Brush electrical equipment whereas the Class 45s had Crompton Parkinson generators and traction motors. Both used 12-cylinder 2,500hp Sulzer 12LDA28B diesel engines. This July 1974 view shows the old order at Newquay with a very tired and neglected-looking No 46005 heading train 1A15, the 10.30 departure to Paddington, while another holiday train can be seen on the left. Meanwhile the local DMU at platform 1 will provide a stopping service to Par. The locomotive worked only to Plymouth, whereupon it returned with the 09.50 Paddington to Newquay.

It is hard to believe that the delightful granite Victorian Newquay station building, seen here, outrageously was demolished only three years after this photograph was taken in October 1987, thus removing an important part of Newquay's limited heritage and an 1876 building of huge historic significance in the development of the town. Standing at what was then the main platform is two-car four-wheeled 'Skipper' unit No 142025, which will shortly leave for Par. These units were remarkably unsuccessful in Cornwall because the wheel flanges squealed on tight curves, the units were not fitted with sanding gear, necessary on steep gradients in wet weather, and their sliding doors were unreliable.

The weekend of 3 and 4 October 1987 has become indelible in the annals of the history of the Newquay branch line. Not only was it the last weekend of the summer timetable but it was the last weekend of semaphore signalling at the Cornish terminus. From Monday 5 October only one train at a time could be accommodated at Newquay, with the nearest passing loop being located at distant Goonbarrow Junction. Locomotive-hauled trains would become a thing of the past, unless they were 'topped and tailed'. To commemorate the event British Rail commendably organised a special train from Paddington on the Sunday, headed by a gleaming pair of Network SouthEast Class 50s, Nos 50034 *Furious* and 50035 *Ark Royal*, seen here at the terminus of the 'Atlantic Coast Line'. Note the yellow wheel-bearing covers.

In this wonderful time warp at Newquay the much lamented days of frequent locomotive-hauled seaside holiday trains are depicted. With semaphore signals and the third Newquay signalbox in full operation one of the classic Class 52 'Westerns', No D1009 *Western Invader*, will shortly be heading up country with train 1E22, the 10.10 SO Newquay to Newcastle. Photographed in June 1974, the locomotive would be withdrawn in November 1976 after a life of only 14 years. The stock for a later train can be seen in the sidings in the background, far removed from the present single-line stub.

It is a desperate railway photographer who stands on the unstaffed Newquay station platform at 20.20 hours on a cold and very wet evening in November! In former Wessex Trains maroon pictogram livery No 150265 forms the last train of the day, the 20.25 Newquay to Par, on 10 November 2008. The scene is greatly enhanced by the wet platform, the photographic technique used being a short time-exposure with the camera pushed against a lamp standard with the addition of fill-in flash. Little imagination is needed to estimate the number of passengers using the train. Note the anti-pigeon/seagull 'spikes' on top of the lamp standard.

As already mentioned, the main interest in motive power on the Newquay branch in recent years has been the liveries of the various TOCs and the trains that they sometimes hire in. For a couple of seasons Virgin Trains made use of GNER and Midland Main Line High Speed Train sets and on 8 September 2007 one of the former units was forming the 09.40 Newquay to Newcastle, seen leaving the terminus with a burst of exhaust as it starts its journey along the single track. Both the GNER and Cross Country franchises changed hands shortly afterwards, creating another piece of modern railway history.

In 2008/9 the new franchise holder Arriva Trains had been busy repainting its IC125 units into 'XC' livery and a very smart No 43304 is seen here passing the delightful ungated Trencreek crossing at 10mph, on 30 May 2009, with the 09.30 Newquay to Newcastle. The crossing once had manually controlled gates operated for many years by Doris Curnow, who still lives in the adjacent crossing-keeper's cottage. Another delightful lady, Gladys Sleeman, once operated the gates at nearby Quintrell Downs. Flashing coloured lights are the impersonal replacement.

In June 1998 RES Class 47/7 No 47765 *Ressaldar*, in one of the more colourful Class 47 liveries, is seen running through St Austell station with an empty stock St Blazey to Penzance postal working, which would return loaded much later in the day. After seven years of operation and having spent millions on special infrastructure, the Post Office announced their virtual abandonment of carrying the mails by rail. Costs, timekeeping and reliability as well as flexibility were cited as reasons for the radical decision and as a bonus their services would, in future, not be susceptible to industrial action by rail unions. Casualties would include the time-honoured Royal Mail 'Travelling Post Office'. The locomotive started life at Crewe in January 1965 as No D1643, later 47059, 47631 and finally 47765. After 40 years of service the locomotive was privately preserved in mid 2005.

110

Since it was opened in 1859 St Austell station has undergone many changes. In 1999 the wooden down side station building was demolished and replaced with a functional but unattractive structure. In 2012 the up building was boarded up, waiting for refurbishment. However, a wonderful survivor is the 1882 GWR passenger overbridge, which dominates this view.

In 2002 the first of the Virgin Voyagers arrived in Cornwall but five years later Virgin would lose the Cross Country franchise. Featured here is a down train in 2004. Note the red sections of overbridge, the red surround to the train cab and the red trousers!

An immense variety of Class 47s have appeared at St Austell over the years. At the last count the class of 512 locomotives had been painted in 300 different liveries over a period of 47 years! However, since privatisation the surviving Class 47s have received a further range of colour schemes, some of them emerging from so-called 'spot hire' companies, such as Cotswold Rail. Many of these companies have regular traffic but covering for failures and special one-off loads is their bread and butter. A rare sight in Cornwall on 3 October 2006 was the now defunct Cotswold Rail's No 47813 *John Peel*, seen here approaching St Austell with a rake of condemned slurry wagons from Burngullow and destined initially for Gloucester but ultimately for scrapping.

It is possible in the summer months to photograph in daylight the down 23.45 Paddington to Penzance sleepers that includes some standard coaches. With the early morning sun rising GM-engined Class 57 No 57603 *Tintagel Castle* is seen ariving at St Austell spot on time with its seven-coach train, on 29 June 2011. The FGW Class 57 fleet are kept in immaculate condition and early reliability issues have largely been overcome.

In addition to some quite glorious countryside Cornwall also has its share of industrial installations. Few are as spectacular as the enormous china clay silos at the former clay dries at Burngullow. Surprisingly this vast storage facility has been disused for many years, although the massive concrete structures survive. Waiting for the Polybulk wagons in the background to be loaded in February 1988 is No 50001 *Dreadnought* in revised Network SouthEast livery. It is hard to believe that the French company Imerys stopped drying clay at the huge site in 2003 and loading ceased altogether in 2008. The occasional sand train continues to be loaded nearby.

Except for the Travelling Post Office the most impressive of the van, postal and perishables trains running through Cornwall in the daylight hours was 3S15, the up Penzance to Glasgow parcels. The train always loaded heavily and was sometimes double headed. In later years it stopped for loading only at Truro and St Austell. This all blue Class 47/4 is seen at the latter location in 1988; note all the BRUTE trolleys along the up platform.

Just to the west of the 207yd-long St Austell Viaduct are the old, abandoned china clay kilns of Trenance and Carroncarrow. Closed in the 1960s, the brick-topped granite stack was covered in ivy when photographed on 1 April 1986 and the roof of the main building was in a state of disrepair. Thundering past the site is No 50009 *Conqueror* with the 09.36 Liverpool Lime Street to Penzance, as seen through a long focal length lens. The Lansalson or Bojea branch once ran northward along the Trenance Valley, which is just visible to the left beyond the larger distant building.

One of the major landmarks to the west of St Austell is the curved 1898-built 115 feet-high St Austell Viaduct, a replacement for an 1859 Brunel/Brereton example that had a wooden upper superstructure. The stone cutters and masons of the rebuilding era earned just 3d per hour! With the piers of the original viaduct still visible No 50047 *Swiftsure* heads west with a down local for Penzance in April 1987, with a single IC coach spoiling the otherwise grey and blue symmetry. The passengers will be getting a wonderful view of the town from their mobile vantage point.

To capture wonderful winter lighting such as that seen here it is necessary to photograph Cornish railways in all seasons of the year. Backlit by the setting sun is No 66174 on a bitterly cold 1 February 2012 as it passes Burngullow with the returning weekly Long Rock to St Blazey empty oil tanks. Two loaded wagons of china clay that had originated at Parkandillack would be added to the train at the adjacent Blackpool sidings. Note the ice encrusted puddle in the foreground and the old stack of the abandoned Burngullow West clay dries in the background.

Back in 1988/9 English China Clays spent some £2 million redeveloping the complex at Burngullow in readiness for a new traffic flow of china clay slurry to the Caledonian Paper Company at Irvine in Scotland. Track reconfiguration and new loading equipment were part of the improvements. From that time the site became known as 'Blackpool' Driers, the name of the large clay pit to the north. Leaving the main line and passing the complex on 4 October 2007 is a late-afternoon working from Carne Point to Parkandillack powered by No 66019. In the sidings is the ex-BR Class 08 shunter No P400D *Susan*, formerly No 08320, which has become redundant following the closure of the site.

One of the most interesting and exciting episodes in Cornish modern traction history was in 1987 when Railfreight decided to change the gearing of a Class 50 locomotive, effectively sacrificing speed for tractive effort. The selected locomotive, No 50049 *Defiance*, was repainted in triple grey Railfreight livery and renumbered 50149. The nameplate had a yellow background.

After trials in the Westbury area the locomotive was despatched to Cornwall where it spent most of its days on china clay train duty before re-conversion during 1989. The unique machine is seen coming off the Drinnick Mill branch at Burngullow with a couple of 'Tiger' wagons in February 1988. On the left is a reminder of the long-closed Burngullow station.

The long 1Co-Co1 Class 45/46 'Peaks' were most associated in Cornwall with long-distance freight trains, particularly to Stoke on Trent and Mossend in Glasgow. However, once at St Blazey they were often put out to the branches on various trip workings. By 1985 their days were numbered in the Royal Duchy and it was therefore especially satisfying to find No 45072 at work on the Drinnick Mill branch on 18 April of that year. With a clay waste mountain as a backdrop the 133-ton (135 tonnes) machine passes below the villages of Foxhole and High Street with a Cargowaggon (sic) and three Tigers as it runs downhill towards the main line at Burngullow.

A short distance from the junction at Burngullow was Crugwallins clay dries, which sadly closed towards the end of 2007 as part of a general downturn in the china clay industry. In happier days during May 1993 some wagons have been deposited in the siding for loading while No 37673 descends the 1 in 50 towards the main line with CDA wagons from Treviscoe to the docks at Fowey. Crugwallins had a resident shunting locomotive to pull the wagons forward.

While the photographers of yesteryear must be admired for carting their heavy and cumbersome equipment cross-country they must also be criticised for being more inclined to photograph the 'Cornish Riviera Express' than a humble, industrial clay siding. This has resulted in a scarcity of photographs of obscure lines from times past. Another problem encountered in the old days was transport, where only the more affluent enthusiasts could afford a car. By the time equipment and domestic circumstances changed many of the more obscure lines had closed. One siding that survived until 1992 ran from Drinnick Mill down to Nanpean Wharf and after reversal, Carloggas, and the lower Drinnick lines. Photographed from the 'main' branch line on 22 July 1986 is No 37696 shunting HEA coal wagons, which were part of a 'Speedlink' service. The coal was for domestic ECC use but also for local distribution. The route of the access line is now a veritable forest and unbelieveably all of the buildings visible here have since been demolished.

This busy scene at Kernick clay driers dates back to 5 May 1989. New Railfreight coloured No 37673 has left five 'Tiger' wagons on the main branch temporarily while it indulges in a little shunting before taking its full load onwards to Burngullow and St Blazey Yard. Note the sidings set in concrete. There were normally two freight train workings per day on the branch but traffic can be very erratic depending on customer demand, the state of storage levels and shipping conditions. The recent recession and a consequent cut-back in production have hardly helped traffic volumes. In 2012 a train was booked onto the branch on Mondays, Wednesdays and Fridays only with occassional CDA extras.

If ever a picture epitomised Cornish china clay country, this is it. Some have described the Hensbarrow Downs area northwest of St Austell as a moonscape and years ago the countryside, houses and roads (and some say the inhabitants!) were white with china clay dust. The rivers ran white before the environment became more of an issue. In this unrepeatable scene from October 1987, with clay excavation, pipelines and chimneys all about, a very sick No 37412 *Loch Rannoch* powers its nearly 1,000-tonne load away from Kernick and passes Rostowrack in readiness for gradients ahead as severe as 1 in 80/42/34/50. The locomotive had arrived from Eastfield, Glasgow, the previous day, presumably without an MOT certificate! (Notice the Highland terrier on the bodyside – had Laira been 'sold a pup'?)

The steeply graded Drinnick Mill branch should more appropriately be called by its original name, the Newquay & Cornwall Junction Railway. The line opened from Burngullow to Drinnick Mill in 1869 as a broad gauge line and from St Dennis Junction to Drinnick Mill in 1874 as a standard gauge line, eventually becoming standard gauge throughout in 1892.

The line beyond Parkandillack, seen here, to St Dennis Junction was closed and lifted in 1966. Seen 136 years after opening, one wonders what the Victorians would have made of EWS/DBS No 66171, positioning CDA wagons at the Imerys works in April 2010. The town of St Dennis is perched on the hillside in the distance.

Left: In Cornish railway circles some traditions linger for decades. Although the by-then daily Truro to St Blazey goods was nearing the end of its life, the St Blazey supervisors still referred to the train as the 'West Cornwall'. With but a single VDA wagon full of Newquay Steam Beer in tow, a rare bird in Cornwall in the shape of 'generator' Class 47 No 47407 *Aycliffe*, is seen at Burngullow in April 1987. The down line between here and Probus had been lifted by British Rail the year before as an economy measure and 17 years later the long single track section would be expensively reinstated by Railtrack (now Network Rail). The signalbox closed in 1986 and after a period of use by permanent way staff it was mysteriously burnt to the ground.

Right: With all trace of the former down track removed, the old Burngullow signalbox razed, ivy all but obliterating the old up station building and unchecked foliage taking over the entire scene, one could be excused for thinking that this had always been a section of single-track main line. Alstom/General Motors 2,980hp No 67024 breasts the summit of the long climb up from Truro in September 2003 with an empty postal train destined for St Blazey for servicing. The Class 67s still occasionally appear in Cornwall on the Royal Train and on Chartex specials to Par or St Austell, where passengers are often transferred to the now famous Eden Centre by bus. On the right is the freight-only Drinnick Mill branch to Parkandillack.

Left: Having been redoubled in 2004, by the time this photograph was taken in June 2011 the main line track layout at Burngullow was firmly re-established in its pre-1987 configuration. Hammering along the main line and making glorious music DRS Class 37s Nos 37229 and 37409 are about to reach the summit of the line from Truro with returning chartex 1Z38 from Penzance to the Birmingham area. It was great to see the class at work in Cornwall over a decade after their displacement.

Although only dating back to 24 August 1985 there is a sense of nostalgia in this picture, possibly because the 'Peaks' and most of the older Mark 1 rolling stock on the main line disappeared at about that time. Also, seemingly as a precursor to line singling, note that the down road has new flat-bottomed clipped track and good ballast, whereas the up line comprises old bullhead rail with chairs. On a lovely day beside an inviting rural road No 45144 *Royal Signals* passes the village of Coombe, south of St Stephen, with a Penzance to Leeds working. These 16-wheeled monsters added variety to the motive power scene and were much missed on the rail routes of Cornwall.

Nearly a quarter of a century later, with an equally splendid Cornish summer's day on 2 June 2009, a broadly equivalent inter-regional train of the 21st century passes the same spot. How increasing numbers of rail travellers can cram into a four-car Voyager compared with 10 Mark 1 coaches is a mystery and equates to the planning of the madhouse. An attractive

Class 220 unit in its glowing new 'Cross Country' livery works past Coombe with the 09.40 Penzance to Manchester Piccadilly. It is hard to believe that for 17 of the intervening years the track here was single, otherwise the main difference between the two photographs is the remarkable unchecked tree growth and a change in fencing materials.

For a few years in the 1980s many local trains in Cornwall between Plymouth and Penzance, plus the few that started from Exeter, were locomotive-hauled. Part of the rationale was the utilisation of locomotives and stock that had become available through the introduction of IC125 units and subsequent decanting. These were halcyon days for railway enthusiasts and photographers! In this wonderful and typically Cornish scene No 50005 *Collingwood* crosses the superb Coombe St Stephen viaduct with a Penzance to Plymouth train on 4 April 1986. Note the ivy-covered piers of the old viaduct on the left, which was abandoned in 1886.

Below: It's springtime in Cornwall, the daffodils and narcissus are in bloom and there is a hint of green appearing on the trees. On a glorious April day in 2010 an FGW IC125 speeds across Tregarne Viaduct between Truro and St Austell on its way from Penzance to Paddington. There seems little doubt that the class will celebrate their 40th year of operation in the Royal Duchy in 2019.

Until the Class 20/9s started working the annual Chipman's weedkilling trains in the early 1990s, Class 20 locomotives were virtually unknown in Cornwall. However, from time to time the entrepreneurial inclinations of railtour operators result in Chartex motive power visiting locations that are unusual stamping grounds for a particular class. An absolute 'must' for the photographer was the Pathfinder Tours 'Chopper Topper' special. Making a most unusual sight at Lower Dowgas, a few miles west of Burngullow, are Nos 20054 and 20011 on 8 June 1986 as the special heads west. Note the special bracing at this point, necessary to add strength to the track as a result of old, abandoned underground mine workings. Truro will be the next stop.

One of the victims of the purge on lightly used Cornish main line stations in 1964 was Grampound Road. It is strange to relate that over 100 years earlier Lord Falmouth had asked for the down 'express train' (there were only three trains per day each way) to stop at this location but the Cornwall Railway surprisingly refused, saying that the train could not be delayed. With just a trace of the old up platform in situ No 50045 *Achilles* rounds the curve and speeds westward with the down Liverpool to Penzance working on 29 August 1986. What is intriguing is the glimpse of the high clay tips near St Austell in the far distance, top right.

The City of Truro is dominated by two vast railway viaducts, the 1,290ft long Truro Viaduct and the 792ft long Carvedras Viaduct. As seen over the rooftops of Truro, a Trans-Pennine liveried Class 158 and a Class 153 unit forming an up local train are seen crossing the former in March 2007. The unusual viewpoint was accidentally discovered on parking the car for a study visit to the nearby Royal Institute of Cornwall. The cathedral on the right was not completed until 1910 and in terms of wildlife a total of 20 seagulls seem to be in attendance! Truro once had two other stations: Truro Road, the original terminus of the West Cornwall Railway at Highertown (1852 to 1855); and their second terminus at Newham, south of the city. The latter was open to passengers only from 1855 to 1863, although the site survived for freight use until 1971.

With a modest population of 21,000 the City of Truro is the capital of Cornwall and the junction for the Falmouth branch. In 2008 over one million passengers used the station, the busiest in Cornwall with a significant catchment area. This compares with the 29 million travellers that use Paddington each year. In terms of railway infrastructure it was once an important location with ample sidings, goods yard, engine shed, multiple signalboxes, three through-platforms and the place where, from 1859, the broad gauge Cornwall Railway from Plymouth met the standard gauge West Cornwall Railway from Penzance. Arriving at the station with train 1C04, the 12.40 SO Penzance to Cardiff in July 1974, is 2,700hp diesel hydraulic No D1012 *Western Firebrand*, with the Falmouth branch train in the bay on the left.

This is another example of a recent 2007 photograph that demonstrates railway history is perpetually in the making. In what is already 'old' First Great Western livery and fitted with the 'old' and now replaced Paxman Valenta engine, power car No 43042 heads the 08.45 Penzance to Paddington of 1 October 2007, a train that took one minute under five hours for the 305¼-mile journey, an average of just over 62mph (100kph). All of the trains on the departures/arrivals boards are on time except the 11.44 departure of the Exmouth to Penzance train, which on this day was running 6 minutes late. Many down trains have ridiculously slack timings between St Erth and Penzance, almost guaranteeing an 'on time' or even early arrival.

133

This view shows the west end of the Truro station complex on 9 June 1990. By this time a number of Class 47s had been painted in Network SouthEast livery and several of the big Sulzers were allocated to Old Oak Common depot in London. Consequently WR locomotive diagrams of the mid 1980s to early 1990s resulted in NSE appearances in Cornwall, especially on time-dated summer extras. With the driver impatiently leaning out of his cab, revised NSE liveried No 47583 *The County of Hertfordshire* has the road for Penzance with the 11.02 ex-Paddington.

A study in ancient and modern at Truro with the old lower quadrant semaphore signals and the traditional surviving GWR signalbox contrasting with the automatic crossing barriers and the 1989-92 BREL Derby-built Class 158. These 77-tonne 800hp units are quite lively with a maximum speed of 90mph, much faster than the main line speed limit in any part of Cornwall. Alphaline liveried No 158871 approaches the city with the 05.21 Bristol Temple Meads to Penzance working on a dull 1 October 2007. It is hard to believe that these units are already 20 years old.

Although photographs of special trains have been kept to a minimum within these pages, locomotive workings on the Falmouth branch are few and far between, hence the inclusion of another photograph of the 'Chopper Topper' tour of June 1986. The Class 20s had been replaced at Truro by the flagship of the Cornish Railways fleet, No 37207 *William Cookworthy*; note the front-end insignia. In 1985 a certain amount of operational and financial autonomy was extended to Cornish railway management, effectively a precursor to future sectorisation and, as it would transpire, privatisation. The Peter Watts/Pathfinder Tours special is seen leaving Truro for Falmouth Docks with the ugly modern County Hall building in the background, which the Duke of Cornwall (the Prince of Wales and heir to the throne) would certainly not approve of. Cornwall became a Dukedom in 1337.

With a remarkable knack for stating the obvious, an old Cornish signalman acquaintance of the author would always utter the words 'tiz rainin'' in climatic conditions, such as those visible here at Penryn on 8 September 2005. At a heavily rationalised station four passengers are about to board 'Super Sprinter' unit No 153382, which is on its way from Falmouth Docks to Truro. Several ex-Wessex (and Arriva Trains Wales) units were painted in this black and gold 'Scenic Lines Devon and Cornwall' livery, sponsored by the Devon and Cornwall Rail Partnership. In May 2009 a passing line arrangement was made ready for service at Penryn in order to increase line capacity and therefore service frequency (see page 9). Presently there is a half-hourly service on the branch, the best ever on what is locally known as 'The Maritime Line'.

This blaze of colour in March 2007 features Cornwall's native gorse bushes, which bloom and are at their best in early Spring but which retain some of their flowers for many, many subsequent months. Add to that the colour of the Carnon River, a two-car Class 150/2 Wessex Trains DMU crossing the splendid Carnon Viaduct plus a solitary dog-walker, and the beauty of the Cornish landscape can be appreciated. Just visible are the old piers of the original Margery Class A viaduct, built in 1863, which lasted until 1933. The new viaduct cost £40,000 (about £2 million today) 77 years ago. From 1826 until 1915 the old, narrow gauge Redruth & Chasewater Railway ran down the Carnon Valley and beneath the viaduct from the Gwennap mines area to the old port of Devoran.

An interesting impression of the Falmouth Docks terminus in July 1999 featuring a wide angle, rather than a telephoto, lens. In the foreground are a couple of old fish-plates and the 312½-milepost, which represents the mileage from London but via Bristol and Plymouth Millbay, pre-dating the 1906 Berks & Hants 'cut-off' route. In the background a Class 150/2 stands at the surviving awning while on the left is the weed-covered connection to what was once an extensive docks railway network. In this area there was once a very fine station building with an all-over-roof, several stock and goods sidings, a goods yard and shed, a signalbox, an engine shed and a turntable, but that is now all a matter of history.

For those who remember 'the old days' it seems inconceivable that with the exception of the up and down overnight sleepers there is now only one locomotive-hauled train per week west of Burngullow, the working that comprises fuel tankers for use by the railway at Long Rock depot, east of Penzance. The day of operation seems to change regularly but at this time it was a Fridays-only working (presently Wednesdays-only). Leaving the 47yd Redruth Tunnel and passing the largely unspoilt station is No 66199 on 23 May 2008 on its down run. The tanks originate at Fawley in Hampshire, the empties from the previous week forming the backload.

With the exception of the Royal Albert Bridge over the River Tamar, the old Hallenbeagle Mine engine-house near Scorrier has, arguably, become the greatest Cornish railway photographic icon, primarily because this remarkable relic is the nearest such survivor to the Cornish main line. Prior to closure in 1963 this was also the site of Great Wheal Busy siding, which effectively was the Scorrier station goods yard. Galloping by and scaring the local bird population in the process is No 50025 *Invincible* with a down express for Penzance comprising a curious mix of Mk 1, Mk 2a and Mk 2e coaches, in August 1985.

There was some good fortune on 8 April 2009 when the weekly Long Rock to St Blazey empty fuel-tank train was running about one hour late, allowing the sun to move sufficiently to provide wonderful backlighting to both the train and the stunning gorse bushes that were in full bloom. In this typical West Cornwall scene No 66172 was setting a fair pace on the up main line with its short train of empties as it passed a 'sound warning' sign on the down road. The sign reminds drivers that there is a pedestrian crossing across the track almost opposite Hallenbeagle mine, which stands gauntly against the skyline.

In the era of InterCity branding, which was applied to many UK primary express trains running over what were ostensibly still British Rail metals, this named, IC liveried but unidentified Class 47/4 is seen passing the industrial wastelands at Tuckingmill east of Camborne in September 1988 with an 11-coach express from Penzance. This area was once infested by mines extracting copper, lead, tin and arsenic with by-products including zinc and wolfram. The stacks of engine houses covered much of the landscape but since the mid and late 19th century the mines have gradually closed and many of the structures razed, just two abandoned engine houses being visible in this shot.

Hayle station is now a shadow of its former self with everything except two primitive waiting huts, the basic platform and some lighting having been stripped away. The wonderful signalbox that controlled the main line and the branch down to Hayle Wharf was demolished in the 1980s and the station overbridge, buildings and goods shed have long since disappeared. The driver of long-range fuel-tanked, IC liveried No 47850 makes a spectacular contribution to the pollution of the atmosphere as this 100-tonne 'two coaches and a van' local, forming the 13.30 Penzance to Plymouth of 24 September 1993, leaves Hayle. Note the viaduct in the background.

Camborne has the largest population in West Cornwall and in times past the town was the epicentre of wealth creation in the county. However, if judged by the facilities at the current railway station its importance is underestimated, although a buffet service was recently reinstated for the 194,000 passengers using the station each year. Local traffic looks buoyant in this October 2007 scene as about 30, mainly young, people leave what must have been a very crowded No 150239. A miserable bus shelter provides basic creature comforts on the down platform while the awning once attached to the fine brick building on the up side has been removed and yet another glass and alloy shelter provided. There is no GWR 'fire in the waiting room' here but at least the passengers on the up side are able to sit on ex-GWR station seats!

Since the end of working steam in Cornwall in 1962 and the last steam special in 1964 it was some decades before preserved main line steam took to the Cornish rails. Since then there have been numerous steam-hauled specials hauled by an immense variety of locomotive classes. Although *Cornish Railways* focuses on the working railway rather than chartex traffic it would be unrepresentative not to include at least one shot of these remarkable trains. In this 'steam and gorse' photograph the most unusual 4-6-2 Pacific pairing of 'Battle of Britain' class No 34067 *Tangmere* and 'Britannia' class No 70013 *Oliver Cromwell* is featured, hauling the prestigious 'The Great Britain 11' tour from Penzance to Scotland on 7 April 2009. The train is climbing the 1 in 83/74 up to Angarrack Viaduct east of Hayle, accompanied by a strong 'southwester'.

This quite wonderful Cornish scene is simply oozing with atmosphere. Under a typical Cornish sky, the picture includes the upper part of Angarrack village, some grazing cows in a nearby field, the warm tones of the rebuilt 1885 100ft-high, 720ft-long Angarrack Viaduct and a wonderful field of daffodils that have been grown commercially. As if that was not sufficient, add maroon Class 52 No D1015 *Western Champion* heading an all-maroon rake of stock and the picture is complete. On 7 April 2009 the DTG's fine diesel hydraulic is seen working the Bristol to Penzance leg of 'The Great Britain 11' tour, on time of course! Within a few weeks the locomotive would also be visiting the Kyle of Lochalsh in Scotland.

With the paucity of locomotive-hauled trains in the west of Cornwall, especially since the withdrawal of postal and van trains some years ago, the photographic pursuit of the weekly Long Rock tanks has been a 'must do' activity for the railway enthusiast/photographer. Crossing the spectacular Angarrack Viaduct, which spans the village of the same name, on its return working to Tavistock Junction is Transrail Class 37 No 37673 in June 1997. As with most freight workings there is a booked path for the train but it is common for it to run up to an hour either side of 'right time'. With the closure of signalboxes and the withdrawal of station staff, information is hard to come by, except for those 'in the know', and quite often a long wait is involved to secure a photograph.

One of the most famous non-passenger train workings in Cornwall during the previous century was the 'Travelling Post Office'. This train took the mails from Paddington to Penzance and vice versa nightly, also serving major intermediate points. Some of the mail was sorted en route and it was also possible to stand on certain platforms and post a letter through a postbox-sized aperture in the side of one of the coaches. The author remembers performing this ritual at Bodmin Road. The train normally left Penzance at about 19.20 and in the height of summer it was possible to photograph the train in West Cornwall. On a delightful evening in June 1997 RES Class 47 No 47772 catches the light as it crosses Hayle Viaduct with the distinctive all-red train. Sadly the foreground wharves are now empty, all commercial traffic having vacated the port many decades ago.

Another view of what was then the weekly Burngullow to Long Rock fuel tank train is justified in the quest for locomotive-hauled trains in West Cornwall. In the interests of maximum utilisation of assets the down working in 2007 originated at Burngullow, the locomotive having worked a morning train up to Parkandillack and back. The train had previously worked directly from Tavistock Junction and in more recent times the train started from St Blazey. In 2012 it reverted to being a Burngullow starter. With semaphore signals still extant on 10 September 2007 No 66228 rumbles through St Erth just after breakfast with the up empties.

The fact that lower quadrant semaphore signals survive at seven locations in Cornwall is a remarkable phenomenon in the 21st century. Although the signalling has GWR origins, most examples are of a Western Region pattern. This delightful example is at the up end of the up platform at St Erth and it features the starting signals for both the up main line and the main line to branch connection. Arriving at the branch platform from St Ives on 6 April 2009 is two-car diesel unit No 150244, while in the refuge siding is a Colas Rail track machine. The 1894 signalbox can just be glimpsed above the HST sign, on the up side of the main line. In 2011 the aesthetic appearance of the gantry was spoilt by the erection of an ugly 'Health and Safety' cage around the upper access ladder.

The majority of Class 47s were delivered in a pleasant two-tone green livery with small yellow warning panels. Later, full yellow cab ends were applied for safety/visibility reasons. By July 1974 most of the class had been repainted in BR blue but locomotives that had not visited the works for some time soldiered on in ever deteriorating two-tone green. Here a very grubby No 1646 (originally D1646 and later 47062, 47545 and 97545), showing an incorrect down train headcode, enters St Erth (junction for the St Ives branch) with an up train.

This miserable, wet but atmospheric scene from November 1974 shows one of the best-known of Cornish freight commodities of the era, the up 6A19 St Erth to Acton milk. Over the years millions of gallons of milk were transported from Cornwall to the capital by rail. The primary collection locations were St Erth, Dolcoath, Lostwithiel and Saltash. The milk was conveyed in glass-lined, 3,000-gallon, six-wheeled tankers. Having shunted the yard at St Erth, Class 52 diesel hydraulic No D1047 *Western Lord* would soon be leaving with the up train. St Erth station has seen surprisingly few changes during the past 35 years and, except for the now-felled telegraph posts, the view is very similar today.

All of the Cornish branch lines are photogenic and the St Ives branch is no exception. The line is marketed as 'The St Ives Bay Line'. These two photographs show two generations of diesel multiple-units that have worked the St Erth to St Ives branch arriving at Lelant, although in both cases and despite the passage of time two-car units were deemed to be adequate for the loadings of the day. Remarkably, there are presently 28 round-trip workings on weekdays, one every half-hour for much of the day, but only 10 stop at Lelant and then by request. There is a Sunday service in the summer months. This DMU meets the incoming tide as it heads for St Erth.

The line is so popular that in 1978 a 'park and ride' scheme was introduced whereby motorists parked their cars some 4 miles from St Ives and then travelled by train to the picturesque resort via the newly opened Lelant Saltings station. The original Lelant station seen here is located on the rim of the Saltings, opposite Hayle, although the former station building is now privately owned and the present railway architecture comprises a simple bus shelter. Entering this pretty scene at low tide on 3 June 2009 is an FGW Class 150/2, also making its way to the junction at St Erth.

It is the end of the 2008 season on Porthminster Beach at St Ives and the summer is nearly over. Those hardy souls braving the beach require jackets or at least a windbreak to retain a modicum of comfort. Few will be attempting a paddle. Bringing the late holiday-makers to the attractive port and crossing St Ives Viaduct is FGW refurbished Class 150/2 No 150247, with some of the passengers no doubt using the aforementioned 'park and ride' scheme and letting the train take the strain. Traditional guest houses and 'bed and breakfast' terraces overlook the putting green and the white sands. The line was listed for closure under Dr Beeching's 1963 Reshaping of BR Plan but happily it survived the purge.

In 1877 the St Ives branch was the last in Cornwall to be constructed to the CR/GWR broad gauge but in common with all other broad gauge lines it was converted to standard gauge in 1892. This March 1969 view shows the fine original granite station building, which was sadly demolished to make room for a substantial and subsequently lucrative car park. The new, simple station was located further away from the town; great for motorists but less convenient for rail passengers. An all-blue, two-car diesel mechanical unit waits to leave for St Erth over 40 years ago. The trackbed on the right is a leftover from the days of steam and was once part of the locomotive run round loop.

An unusual stretch of the Cornish main line is between the closed station at Marazion and a few hundred yards short of the Penzance terminus. The former double track section was singled in 1974 in the interests of economy, enabling a signalbox to be closed. Other than for the Royal Albert Bridge and a short section of track over St Pinnock and Largin Viaducts, this is the only other stretch of single track on the Cornish main line, and it seems to be hugely under-photographed. Passing some modern coastal residences and surrounded by rape-plant flowers, No 66237 approaches Long Rock on 3 June 2009 with the only and already featured, down daytime locomotive working of the week, the St Blazey to Long Rock fuel tanks.

On occasions the delivery of loaded tankers to Long Rock and the collection of empty wagons takes but a few minutes but at other times the locomotive can be in the sidings for an hour waiting a suitable return path. On 3 June 2009 there was a rapid turn round and No 66237 is seen scampering off to St Blazey with half a dozen empties in tow. The train is passing the remains of Marazion station, which closed in 1964, and the up yard where thousands of tons of broccoli were once loaded into railway wagons.

The lines to the left once served goods platforms, a goods shed and even the very first engine shed at Penzance, not to mention Albert Quay along the harbour wall. In comparatively recent times the sidings have been used to stable locomotives but now the car is king and goods traffic and locomotive-hauled trains have all but disappeared, resulting in an extended car park.

In June 1997 RES liveried No 47772 has backed onto the matching stock of the much lamented TPO that would depart at 19.20. Note the BRUTE trolleys used in the transfer of mails and packages in front of the locomotive. For decades, long before the advent of radio or television, folk in the far west of the UK relied on the TPO and the nightly newspaper trains to bring them letters, greetings and bills as well as the world's news, but now it is fibre-optic cables, air waves and roads that provide the service.

Left: A couple of times per day there is a through train from Penzance to St Ives and vice versa but otherwise the branch unit shuttles between St Erth and St Ives all day. On another atrocious day in August 1992 attractive Regional Railways liveried Class 122 'bubble car' No 55012 is coupled to a Class 101 2-car unit, which will shortly leave the terminus for St Ives. A few years ago the station was refurbished and the all-over roof restored. However, no smoke extractors were fitted and Valenta-engined IC125 power cars were obliged to stop short of the roof-covering to prevent passenger asphyxiation upon engine restart! Half a million passengers used Penzance station during 2008.

Left: Again the fair weather photographer would have missed out on this November 1974 opportunity to record a wretched and miserable day at Penzance station when the platforms flooded. One wonders whether the solitary tail lamp might have been extinguished by the deluge! On the left is a rake of air-braked, air-conditioned and electrically heated coaches that the Class 52 'Western' on the right could not have operated in normal service – just one reason for the eventual demise of the class. Despite the headcode, the 'Whizzo' is not about to work a Class 7 train destined for the Eastern Region!

Right: The sight of a pair of Southern Region Class 33/2 'Slim Jims' at Penzance is an extremely rare event but that is what occurred on 22 October 1988 when the 'Cornish Crompton Farewell' visited the town. In appalling weather over 70 enthusiasts face the elements to witness and photograph the novelty. Nos 33211 and 33207 prepare to return the Chartex to Waterloo at 15.18, having arrived just one hour earlier at 14.07. It transpired that this was not to be the last visit to Cornwall for Class 33s (see Page 4).

157

First opened in 1852, Penzance has undergone rebuilding on a number of occasions, including several changes in platform layout and track configuration, with the GWR even building on land reclaimed from the sea. It is refreshing to note that in BR days the station staff had been indulging in some landscape gardening at England's most westerly main line terminus. In this interesting view from October 1975 No D1034 *Western Dragoon* is in the foreground, while a sister locomotive departs the station. Five semaphore signals and three shunting discs complete the colourful scene. This could have been the last photograph taken of *Western Dragoon* in service, as it was withdrawn later in the month.

A timeless view of 'the blocks' at Penzance. Although several classes of visiting motive power have been photographed under the magnificent train shed of Penzance terminus, it seemed more appropriate on this occasion to include this wonderful piece of Swindon-built British engineering (albeit with German engines and transmissions!), the DTG's ex-BR maroon liveried Class 52 'Western' diesel hydraulic No D1015 *Western Champion*. The historic permanence of this traditional granite structure is a fitting penultimate picture of our journey through Cornwall and may it continue to serve future generations for centuries to come. The locomotive had arrived with a chartex special on 7 April 2009 and was photographed with a hand-held 1984 Nikon FE2 film camera, with a 35mm A1 f2 Nikkor lens, using Fuji Superia 200asa film, with a single fill-in flash from a camera mounted 39-year-old National PE-300 flash gun.

... and so the sun went down over the town of Penzance, ending yet another day, and also ending our all-colour photographic railtour of Cornish Railways spanning a period of 43 years, albeit from a very personal perspective. At twilight on an April day in 2009 the good ship *Scillonian* from the Isles of Scilly has just docked, top left, and the last vestiges of daylight silhouette the hills beyond. It is time for the 'Night Riviera' to prepare for its long overnight journey to London, which will commence at 21.45 behind GM-engined Class 57/6 No 57605 *Totnes Castle*, conveying both sleeping-car passengers and the 'wakers' to the capital, over 300 miles distant. 'Proper job!'